SO-BDL-903

BARRON'S
A BUSINESS
SUCCESS GUIDE

Using the Telephone More Effectively

By

Madeline Bodin
Editor
INBOUND/OUTBOUND
MAGAZINE

BARRON'S

DEDICATION

For my husband, Mark

Copyright ©1991 by Barron's Educational Series

All inquiries should be addressed to:
Barron's Educational Series, Inc.
250 Wireless Boulevard
Hauppauge, New York 11788

Library of Congress Catalog Card No. 91-8243

International Standard Book No. 0-8120-4672-2

Library of Congress Cataloging in Publication Data

Bodin, Madeline.
   Using the telephone more effectively / by Madeline Bodin.
       p. cm.—(Barron's business success series)
     ISBN 0-8120-4672-2
   1. Telephone in business. I. Title. II. Series.
HF5541.T4B63 1991
651.7'3—dc20   91-8243
                                                             CIP

PRINTED IN THE UNITED STATES OF AMERICA

'34   5500   98765432

CONTENTS

CONTENTS

CHAPTER 1

INTRODUCTION:

*Acquiring More
Sophisticated Telephone
Skills*

Undoubtedly a man is to labor to better his condition, but first to better himself.

—William Ellery Channing

The sky is falling. Or at least it seems that way to your company. You must get in touch with your top people right away. The first person you call is out of the office. You leave a message, but he never calls back. You can't reach the second person either, so you leave your name and number in her voice mailbox. The third person's secretary gives you his cellular phone number, but the phone just rings and rings. You get back from lunch to find out that the second person returned your call when you were out. The boss wants a conference call, but when you finally get everyone on the line the meeting falls apart.

Does it sometimes seem that instead of helping you manage more effectively, the telephone just gets in your way?

This book tells you how to use the most common and underestimated piece of office technology—the telephone—effectively. You wouldn't dream of using a new computer or a new software package without training, or at least reading the manual. Yet, in the workplace, most people use the telephone with only the training they received as children. As a business person, your communication needs are more sophisticated now. Telephone systems have also become more complicated. Let this book be your telephone users' manual. Good business telephone skills help you avoid misunderstandings, "telephone tag," and unnecessary interruptions in your work.

Every business telephone system has hundreds of features. There are four features that every business person must know how to use: hold, transfer, forward, and speed dial. Other less common but useful features can also help you improve your telephone effectiveness. If your secretary just answers your phone and takes messages, you are not taking full advantage of his or her ability to make you more effective on the telephone.

If you are like many business people, you are skilled at getting past the secretary or assistant who screens an executive's calls. But the most effective tactic is to work with the screener to place your call. When you reach the executive, your well-rehearsed presentation will mark you as an amateur.

Modern telephone selling techniques can help you get your point across even if you are not a salesperson. But what if you don't reach a secretary or an executive? What if you reach an automated attendant and a voice mailbox instead? What if you must talk to the executive by videoconference?

New technology can throw even the most skilled telephone user for a loop. But there are techniques that can make technology work for you instead of against you.

This book will teach you how to:

- prioritize your return calls so they are all returned in time;
- screen your own telephone calls even if you do not have a secretary;
- keep telephone calls on track so callers don't waste your time;
- get in touch with someone after one telephone message, not dozens;
- reach busy or important people by telephone, and salvage the call if you can't;

- sell products and ideas by telephone;
- deal with telephones that are ringing off the hook
- make the best of voice mail—both in your company and when you encounter it at other companies; and
- prepare for a teleconference or videoconference.

You have probably outgrown many office skills. For example, you may no longer type your own letters and someone else may file your reports. You may have delegated your photocopying chores. But you always need telephone skills. They take you right to the top.

CHAPTER 2

BASIC TELEPHONE SKILLS:

What Every Manager Needs to Know

Speech is power: to persuade, to convert, to compel.

—Ralph Waldo Emerson

T he secret to using the telephone effectively is *planning*. However, planning a telephone call seems unnatural to many of us. We are used to picking up the phone to chat with family and friends whenever the mood strikes. Planning a telephone call is unnatural in a social situation. For most of us, using the telephone is a social skill, not a business skill.

The rules differ for business telephone calls. Making a business call requires the same skills as participating in a meeting, sending a memo, or writing a business letter. It requires thought and planning.

You can easily understand how to plan your calls to other people, but you may not think it is possible to plan for other people's calls to you. It is possible, and necessary, to plan for these incoming calls. The first thing to plan is how you will answer your telephone.

ANSWERING YOUR PHONE

Many telephone effectiveness experts feel that the first ten to fifteen seconds of a telephone call set the tone of the entire conversation. It is therefore easy to see why the way you answer your telephone is important. "You should answer your telephone with a couple of key words that let your callers know they have reached the right place," says Gail Cohen, President of the Telemarketing Learning Center and a telephone consultant.

Answering your phone with a brusque "What do you want?" will set a negative tone for the conversation that follows. You must answer your phone with a phrase that is both pleasant and professional.

Nancy Friedman, a St. Louis-based communications consultant who dubs herself "the Telephone Doctor," says this key phrase should contain three things:

- a greeting
- the name of your company or department
- your name

"Hello, Accounting, this is Lynn Johnson," is a suggested greeting that contains all three elements.

The appropriateness of the greeting varies with the type of company you work for, your department, and your personal style. "Hello," "Good morning," or any salutation that agrees with your personal, departmental, and company image can be used.

Friedman says that the greeting also acts as a buffer; that is, it keeps the important information—your department and name—from being clipped from the conversation by speakerphones, long-distance services, or inattentive listeners.

Callers expect to hear a greeting when their call is answered. "Hello" or some other word gives your caller a split second to register that the phone has been answered and to prepare for the information that will follow.

If you have a direct line or your calls do not pass through a receptionist or secretary, include your company name when you answer your calls. If your calls do pass through a receptionist or secretary, include the name of your department in addition to your own name.

For your name, the phrase "This is Lynn Johnson" is preferred to "Lynn Johnson speaking." Gail Cohen says, "Always end with your name. The last thing you say becomes the first thing on the caller's mind."

Another thing to consider in those critical first ten to fifteen seconds is your tone of voice. "If you are having a bad day, or something is bothering you, take the anger out of your voice for fifteen seconds when you pick up the telephone," advises a spokesperson for a major telecommunications company. "This gives you time to set the tone of the conversation."

Cohen suggests using the old telemarketer's trick of putting a mirror near your telephone to make sure you are creating the right impression. "There's no question that your body position and facial expression come across on the phone," she says. A mirror makes you aware of your expression—and therefore of the impression you are making.

CALL SCREENING AND INTERRUPTIONS

Many business people prefer to have all their calls screened. Your secretary or assistant can screen your calls. If you do not have a secretary or an assistant, you may do it yourself.

Call screening has gotten a bad reputation. When we think of call screening, we think of a secretary dedicated to keeping all telephone calls from the boss. But the secretary who takes that approach is not performing call screening effectively. "A secretary should screen calls in, not screen calls out," says Dr. Larry Baker, a time-management consultant and president of the Time Management Center, located in St. Louis. "The objective should be to make sure you get all the important calls."

When You Must Screen Your Own Calls

The first thing you should do when answering your own telephone is to quickly and politely find out what the caller wants. The phrase "How can I help you?" or

"What can I do for you?" quickly brings the caller to the point of the call.

Dr. Baker says you must compare the importance of each phone call to the importance of the work it is interrupting. If the call is not as important, find another person to help the caller. The idea is not to dump the call on someone else but to find someone who can actually assist the caller.

If you are the only one who can help the caller, ask whether you can call him or her back later in the day or on another day when you have more time to help. Give a specific time when you will return the call, and consider it an appointment you must keep. If the caller needs your help immediately, set a time limit so you can get back to your own project quickly. Say something like, "I only have ten minutes. Can we discuss this in that time or should I call you back later?"

When you screen your own calls, says Dr. Baker, one of the hardest things to do is to get rid of total time wasters. "You have to be able to say no without guilt," he says. If something is not in your interest or is not your responsibility, you must say so. According to Baker every phone call you receive can be put into three categories:

- I will talk to them now
- I will talk to them later
- the call is not in my interest or area of responsibility.

Setting Priorities

Dr. Baker's method of placing calls in one of three categories builds on priority-setting skills that are probably second nature to you. It is a helpful formula to help you use those skills to handle screening your own calls with minimum interruption to your work.

Baker suggests using two yardsticks to determine which of the three categories a call fits into: importance and urgency. Most people know when a call is important, but sometimes a call that is not really important must be handled quickly. For example, the mailroom may call you because your overnight package carrier noticed you didn't specify whether you wanted overnight or two-day delivery for a particular package. Is the call important? Perhaps not, but if you don't handle it immediately you may lose the opportunity to decide how the package is sent. The call is urgent but not important.

When you receive a call, you should ask yourself two questions:

1. "Is this call more *important* than what I am doing now?"

2. "Is this call more *urgent* than what I am doing now?"

If you answer yes to either question, the call falls into the "I will talk to them now" category. Unfortunately, things are rarely so simple, notes Baker. The call may be equally important to what you are doing but more urgent. "Time management experts often tell people to set priorities but don't tell them to look at what's best for the team."

If the call is an internal one, you have to look beyond your own priorities to the priorities of the company. If your work is equally important, but the call is more urgent, the company is better off if you cooperate with your caller and put your own work aside for a moment.

But being a team player doesn't mean you have to give in to every interruption. If the call is important but the work you are doing is urgent, ask your caller to wait. "Can I call you back in thirty minutes?" you might ask. Usually the caller will agree. These are the calls in the "I will talk to them later" category.

Of course, there will be times when both you and your caller have urgent tasks. If the call is both important and urgent, you will need to take some action. "Never send a caller away empty-handed who has come to you with a legitimate need or request," says Baker. If the caller can't wait for you to return the call at a more convenient time, you may want to pass him or her on to a co-worker who can help. If no co-worker or other resource can help the caller and his or her request is both important and urgent, Baker feels the most effective time management technique is to stop what you are doing and help the caller. The most effective decision is the one that benefits the company as a whole.

Some telephone calls are of no benefit to your company. When you receive a request that is a waste of time for you or for your company, just say no, you won't handle the call. "Many people have a hard time handling these phone calls," says Baker. "They don't want to be thought of as rude and feel guilty for saying no. But if you think about it, these phone calls don't benefit anyone. You should feel guilty if you *don't* say no."

It's rare, though, that you can just say no to a telephone call. If you are a manager, for example, most of the phone calls you receive are important and will require your attention, if not now, then at some future time. Getting into the habit of *categorizing* your calls can help you minimize disruptions.

WHEN YOU MUST ANSWER A CO-WORKER'S PHONE

As a team player, you may sometimes have to answer a co-worker's phone. When you pick up someone else's phone, greet the caller with that person's name as well as your own. For example: "Hello. Lynn Jones's office. This is Lee Brown." Offer to take a message or to help the caller if you can. Do not try to answer questions when you don't have answers. Some issues, such as product release dates or marketing strategies, are common knowledge within a company but cannot be given to callers outside the company. If you are answering a call for a co-worker in another department where you don't know the policies, limit your assistance to taking a message. Explain to the caller that you don't normally work closely with the person he or she is trying to reach. Offer again to take a message. Remember to get the caller's name, company name, phone number (including area code), and some information on what the call is about. Once you have taken a message, be sure your co-worker receives it.

Prioritize Your Calls

Once you know what the caller wants, decide if it is more important than what you were doing before the call. Telephone effectiveness experts point out that there are *positive interruptions* and *negative interruptions*. It is possible that any given phone call is more important than the paperwork it interrupts.

Of course, if the call is important you should take it immediately. But if the task that was interrupted is more important, you have a number of options:

- arrange to call the person back
- delegate the call to someone else
- say no to a call that will waste your time

You or your secretary can arrange to call the person back at a later time. Be sure to set a specific time to return the call when you are both available.

The call can also be *delegated* to someone else. Many calls that wind up at a manager's desk do not require a manager's attention. Nancy Friedman reports that out of every ten phone calls she receives, eight can be handled by her assistant.

If you delegate a phone call to your assistant, the assistant should let the caller know that he or she works closely with you and can take care of the problem or question. The person to whom you delegate the call, whether it is your assistant or someone else in your department, should be able to help the caller. "Don't just dump them on someone who can't help them," says Baker of Time Management Center.

The third possibility is that the phone call is a total waste of your time. "If the call is not in your interest or area of responsibility you have to be able to say no without guilt," says Baker.

Look for Patterns

It may seem that incoming calls are unpredictable—that you can't tell who will call, when they will call, or what they will say. By keeping a log of your telephone calls, you may find you are able to predict the volume and nature of calls. You may find that the same people call you about the same things at certain times during the day, week, or month.

For example, you may find that salespeople always call the day after the month's sales figures are released. Or you may find that your clients tend to flood you with inquiries on Monday mornings and complaints on Wednesday afternoons. Once you have determined the patterns in the calls you receive, you can arrange your work agenda so that the calls are less disruptive.

THE MOST IMPORTANT TELEPHONE ACCESSORY

Keep a pen or pencil and a supply of paper near your telephone. "I can't imagine a telephone without paper and a pen nearby," says Nancy Friedman, "but I see it often when I go into other people's offices to make a phone call."

When you receive a telephone call, the first thing you should do is jot down the name of the person who is calling. At first a phonetic spelling of the name will do. If you need to follow up with written material or another call, ask for the precise spelling.

Once you have the caller's name, use it to address him or her in the course of the conversation. This lets your caller know you are paying attention and care about the call. Of course, you should be careful not to overdo it. You have probably received calls from people who used your name in every sentence, much as an unctuous used car salesman might.

KEEPING DISORGANIZED CALLERS ON TRACK

When you receive a call, you may have a tendency to be a passive recipient of information. One thing you should do during all telephone calls—those you receive and those you make—is *take notes*. These notes need not be extensive. Jotting down a few key words or phrases helps you keep the conversation on track if the caller digresses. When the call ends, these notes serve as reminders of what was discussed.

Sometimes a disorganized caller will make you disorganized. If there is certain information you need to help callers with common questions—department codes to requisition materials or invoice numbers to track accounts payable, for example—make a list for yourself to be sure you get all the information you need from a disorganized caller. Airline reservation agents are particularly good at this, says Baker. They get callers to give information in the order it is needed.

RECAP EACH CONVERSATION

The details of a conversation tend to become vague soon after the discussion ends. For this reason, at the end of your conversation quickly summarize what was said and decided. "It is unnatural to recap a conversation, but you should be secure enough to do it," says a spokesperson for a major telecommunications company. "If it's worth discussing at length, it's worth a thirty-second recap." The *wrap-up* allows both parties to come away with a clear picture of the purpose of the call and what was accomplished.

RETURNING CALLS

An important part of using the telephone effectively is returning calls. "When you ask a person to leave a message in voice mail or on an answering machine, there is an implied promise that you will return the call," says Baker of the Time Management Center. And when your secretary takes a message, he or she usually assures the caller you will return the call.

Failure to return the call breaks that real or implied promise, and this does not reflect well on you. If you cannot return the call yourself, delegate it to a member of your staff who can. If time is the issue, call back to set a date and time for a longer conversation. If there is any possibility you won't be able to return the call, the best course of action is not to promise to return it in the first place, says Baker.

OUTGOING CALLS

Planning the calls you make to other people is easy. After all, you yourself determine the time, nature, and duration of these calls. But making the conversation a productive one, not only for yourself but for the person you are calling, is another matter.

One key to making the calls you place productive is to be considerate of the time constraints of the people you call. What to you is a quick question in the course of the task at hand may be a needless interruption to the person you are calling.

There are several ways to avoid this problem. You can save up several points that are not urgent and make a single telephone call. At the same time, there may be a person that you must speak to several times a day by telephone, even after you have saved up several points. You may want to schedule a few times each day for calls to and from this person so you are not constantly interrupting each other, suggests Baker.

It is important that both of you make impromptu calls for urgent matters, but save the merely important matters for your scheduled calls cuts down on interruptions for both of you.

SET THE AGENDA

"When you reach someone by phone, you are having a two-person meeting," says Dr. Larry Baker. "Any meeting is more effective with an agenda." It is the caller's responsibility to set the agenda for the telephone call. Having a list of what you want to accomplish along with an awareness of the urgency of each point helps save time and makes your call more effective.

You need not make an elaborate plan for your outgoing calls. Nancy Friedman suggests jotting down just six or eight words that will remind you of what you need to accomplish and keep you on track.

For example, before you call a colleague, you should write a few words on a piece of paper: "Mortimer contract, northwest region, VP dinner." These phrases are your agenda for a call in which you want to discuss your company's contract with the Mortimer Company, your company's expansion into the northwestern United States, and the upcoming retirement dinner for the vice president of finance. You will be able to keep the call on track through these varied topics.

TIPS ON AVOIDING TELEPHONE TAG

Nancy Friedman estimates that seven out of every ten calls you make are not completed: that is, you won't reach the person you were trying to call.

At the very least what you should get out of any telephone call is the time the person you are trying to reach will return or the best time to call back. "The person you ask will probably say they don't know," says Friedman. "Ask them to make a blind guess. They may tell you the person usually picks up messages at 4:30. At least you will have an idea." Also, always leave a message and make sure your message specifies a time for the person to call you back. If you will be in a meeting until noon, leave that in the message. If you know you are available for only two hours that day, one in the morning and one in the afternoon, let the person know what these hours are.

Leaving specific messages that include what time is best to return your call helps eliminate *telephone tag*, the office game where two people take turns leaving messages for each other.

Here are some other ways to avoid this frustration:

1. If the person you are calling has voice mail, leave a message that includes the points on your agenda. If you need the answer to a particular question by a certain time, include that in your message as well. For example, you might leave a voice mail message saying, "I need to speak to you about the Mortimer contract by 5 o'clock today, and we also need to discuss the northwest regional expansion and Terry's retirement dinner."

2. Whenever you leave a message, especially on voice mail, be sure to include your telephone number. Voice mail systems let people pick up their messages when they are out of the office, and although your phone number may be in their files, they won't have the files on hand to call you back immediately.

3. Respect the time of those people you do get in touch with right away. Estimate how long the conversation will last and ask them if they have the time to speak to you immediately. And do not hesitate to set up an appointment to speak at a later time. "When people don't want to talk to you, you don't want to talk to them. If they are in a rush, you will not have a productive conversation," says Gail Cohen.

4. When you set up the appointment, make sure the person knows how urgent the conversation is. If you need an answer to a question by Tuesday, he or she may be willing to clear some time for you on Monday. People you don't tell about your deadline, may say they are not free until Thursday afternoon.

Impromptu calls are best left for emergencies and social situations. A little bit of planning—jotting down the important points that need to be covered during a call, setting a specific time for telephone call-backs, and leaving detailed messages—helps you get a lot more out of each telephone call.

LOOKING AT THE BIG PICTURE

The basic telephone skills you have learned in this chapter are the building blocks of telephone effectiveness. Answering calls with a key phrase that contains a greeting, your department, and your name will help all the calls you receive go more smoothly. Learning to set the tone of a telephone conversation in the first 15 seconds also is helpful for all calls, but will be important especially when you need to make a persuasive call or a sales call.

Getting into the habit of setting an agenda for the phone calls you make—even if it's just a few words jotted on a piece of paper—will assure that you always cover all the points you planned during your call and will save you from making a second phone call. Later, when we discuss voice mail and teleconferencing, we'll see how this skill will help you use two new telephone technologies better.

Scheduling return telephone calls and asking secretaries and co-workers for information on the person you are calling can save time even on routine telephone calls. When you are trying to reach someone who is very busy or important, these skills are crucial.

Although these skills are basic, don't let their simplicity fool you. Turning these skills into habits is not easy, but if you do, they will help you accomplish more on every call.

CHAPTER 3

GETTING TO KNOW YOUR PHONE SYSTEM:

The More You Know, the Better

We live in a time of such rapid change and growth of knowledge that only he who continues to learn and inquire can hope to keep pace, let alone play the role of guide.

—Nathan Pussey (educator)

On your first day of work at a new company you may get a packet that explains your benefits, describes the company's vacation policy, and lists company holidays. You may get a tour of the office and meet your co-workers. And, if you are lucky, you may get an orientation to the company telephone system. You will no doubt be tempted to skip the telephone orientation. After all, you say to yourself, you know how to use a telephone, and there is important work to do.

Learning your new company's phone system is every bit as important as learning its policies and procedures. You may know how to put someone on hold, but do you know how the phone system handles a call that has been put on hold? Some systems are programmed to return the call to the company receptionist. Other systems may transfer the call to your secretary or your phone may ring to remind you that the call is still on hold.

Avail yourself of any telephone training that is offered, whether it is when you start your employment or when a new phone system is installed. Even if you know the basics, you may pick up tips and techniques that enable you to use familiar features better. Or you may learn about new features or programmable options that save you time and effort.

What if your company does not offer telephone training? There are several resources you can use to find out more about your phone system. The first is the telephone *user's guide,* a single sheet of paper or a card—a crib sheet—on using the most common features of the phone system. A user's guide will help you through those first few months with a new phone system and will help new members of your department get up to speed more quickly in the future.

If a user's guide was not included in the company orientation packet and your predecessor did not leave a copy, ask one of your co-workers for a copy. If a guide does not exist, create one of your own after doing a little research. (See the Appendix for a Sample Telephone Manual.)

Don't depend on your co-workers alone when creating your user's guide. Find out who is in charge of your company's telephone system. Large companies may have a telecommunications department to manage the telephone system or a training department that handles all types of employee education. Smaller companies may put the purchasing department, the personnel department, or the office manager in charge of the phone system.

At a large company without established aids for learning the phone system, getting information may be a matter of asking the experts in the telecommunications department and perhaps reading the booklets and manuals they suggest. At a small company you may find yourself reading the system administrator's manual and speaking to the company that sold and installed the phone system.

FINDING OUT ABOUT THE FEATURES

Lori Korn is a consultant with CalTel, a firm that helps companies choose, configure, install, and train employees on telephone systems. Here is her list of the questions that should be asked concerning the most useful telephone features. The answers to these questions vary from system to system. There are even differences from company to company with the same model phone system. Each company customizes the phone system for its own use.

Hold

- Will the system *time out* held calls—transfer the held call somewhere else after a set period of time?
- How long can someone be left on hold before the system times out?
- If a held call is transferred, where does it go?
- If you are on one line and do not answer your other line, what happens to the second call? Does it return to the company receptionist? Your secretary or assistant?

Transfer

- What happens if you transfer a call to another extension and no one answers that extension? Will the phone just ring? Will the call return to you? Will it return to the company receptionist?
- Is there any indication that a call has been transferred from within the company?
- If there is no answer at the other extension when you transfer a call, can you retrieve the call? How can you do that?
- Does the phone system let you have a three-way conference with the person you are transferring and the person you are transferring them to so you can announce the call?

Conference

- How many parties can participate in one teleconference? How many people inside your company? How many outside? (There will be different numbers for each.)

- Can you conference two outside callers together and then drop out of their conversation?
- When two people are on hold waiting for more parties to be added to a conference call, can they speak to each other?
- How do you get back to the conference call if one of the parties you are trying to add does not answer the phone or is unavailable? (For more information on conference calls, see Chapter 9.)

Speed Dial

- Does the system have speed dial numbers that are systemwide? How many? How many digits can the system hold for each number?
- Does the system have group speed dial—numbers in common for your department? Can system speed dial numbers be set aside for department use?
- How do you access speed dial numbers? Are there dedicated buttons on your telephone? an access code? both?
- How many numbers can you have on your personal speed dial list?

Speakerphone

- How is the speaker turned on and off during a phone call?
- Does the system let secretaries and co-workers use the speaker to "voice announce" a call before they transfer it?
- Is there a mute button so callers on voice announce can't hear what is going on in your office?

Forward

- Is the system programmed to automatically transfer calls if they are not answered?
- Can internal calls and external calls be routed differently?

- How are the calls in your department routed?
- Can you forward your calls to voice mail? How is that done?
- Can your secretary override your call forward feature and transfer screened calls to you?
- How will the system remind you that your calls have been forwarded? Is there a visual indication? An audible one?

Modern phone systems have dozens of features. As you learn about the basics, ask questions about the more advanced features. With so many options available, the timesaving feature of your dreams may be waiting for you to discover it. Have you ever wished to be alerted when a busy extension is free without having to stay on the line? That feature is available (for internal calls only) on many phone systems.

USING THE MOST HELPFUL FEATURES

Here are some tips to help you use common features more effectively.

Hold

This is the most basic feature on any business telephone system. You already know how to use it, but keep these things in mind:

- Time passes slowly for the caller on hold. Do not leave callers on hold for more than a few seconds without checking on them.
- There is nothing wrong with calling someone back. It's more polite to call people back than to put them on hold for several minutes.

Transfer

Most phone systems let you blindly transfer calls to another party without checking to see if that party is in.

Don't do it. Many phone systems will let you transfer the call and stay on the line to announce it. Do not expect the caller to start from the beginning with the new person. Explain what has already been said and why you are transferring the call. If your phone system allows you to speak confidentially before the caller is connected, warn your co-worker about any special problems—if the caller has been difficult, for example.

For very important calls Lori Korn recommends that you set up a brief conference call between the three parties to make introductions and assure that the transfer goes smoothly.

Speed Dial

Most people know how to use speed dial to store frequently dialed numbers. But many people do not realize that speed dial has other uses as well. For example, your telephone has several feature buttons, such as hold and transfer. On most systems, you use other features by dialing a code. If this is true of your system, you can program a speed dial button with the access code of a feature you use frequently and have one-button access to that feature. Or you can enter the country and city code for overseas cities you call often, which saves you time dialing all calls to that locality.

Call Forward

This feature allows you to forward your calls to someone who can handle them. It is especially useful if your responsibilities involve dealing with customers. At the very least, brief the person your calls are forwarded to on the information you need to have before you return the call.

And do not forget to deactivate the call forward feature on your phone when you don't need it. "You would be surprised how many calls for telephone repair are caused by people who left their call forward on and forgot about it," says Korn. To avoid that problem, some companies ask their receptionist to clear the system of forwarded phones once a week.

The most important step you can take to learn how to use your company's telephone system effectively is to make an effort to educate yourself about it. Attend training sessions. Read the manual or user's guide. Track down the manual yourself if it is not immediately available. (See Appendix for a Sample User's Manual.)

A few minutes of learning to use your telephone will pay for itself in years of more knowledgeable and effective telephone use.

CHAPTER 4

THE TELEPHONE EFFECTIVENESS TEAM—YOU AND YOUR SECRETARY:

Working Together Can Make You More Productive

The best executive is the one who has sense enough to pick good men to do what he wants done.

—Theodore Roosevelt

I f you are lucky enough to have a secretary or an assistant, you can be a far more effective user of the telephone. A secretary or assistant can screen your calls to make sure important calls get through to you and unnecessary calls do not interrupt your work. A secretary can also *organize* your messages and make sure you have the information you need before making them.

Even a good secretary or assistant needs input and cooperation from you to make the system work to your benefit. It is up to you to set the guidelines that will enable you and your assistants to work together as an efficient telephone team.

CALL SCREENING

Good call screening lets you get important work done without interruption from unimportant calls. Bad call screening alienates your callers and may even keep important calls from reaching you. According to time management consultant Dr. Larry Baker, the most important factor in call screening is the attitude of the secretary. "The secretary must screen calls in, not screen calls out," he says. "Don't take a negative approach to screening calls. Secretaries who think their job is to screen out calls that will interrupt their bosses have the wrong attitude. The secretary must think about making sure the boss gets the calls that are important."

Imagine what would happen if a member of your company's board of directors called your office, and your secretary, hearing an unfamiliar name, said you were unavailable. Because your secretary was screening *out* unfamiliar names instead of screening *in* important calls, the board member would question your competence.

Every secretary should be provided with a list of VIPs that can be broken down to differentiate between those who should be put through no matter what and those who should be put through if you are not in a meeting or rushing to beat a deadline. Your VIP list should include your boss's name and the names of all upper-level management. Also list your personal VIPs— including your husband or wife and your children. This helps spare your loved ones the annoyance of being screened, and it may also save your secretary considerable embarrassment.

Your secretary should also have a list of people to screen out. Make it clear that every caller should be dealt with in a polite and professional manner but that certain individuals have to wait until you have time for them.

Tell your secretary how to deal with salespeople. Do you want to see written materials before you speak to them? Will you call them back at a later time? Should they be referred to the purchasing department?

Make sure your secretary knows routine information:

- your fax number
- the company address
- the names of the people in charge of purchasing and personnel
- special procedures

- subjects that can be handled by a staff member or another department

Each phone call your secretary handles is another call that won't interrupt you. However, there may be certain information you will want to give out yourself, even if it can be handled by your secretary. For example, if you are giving a seminar or a speech, your secretary could handle the RSVPs, since the calls will mostly consist of clerical tasks—checking off lists, recording names and addresses, and so on. But you may want to take some of these calls yourself. This will give you the opportunity to speak to some of the attendees before the event and ask them questions. Doing so may give you a feel for your audience or the effectiveness of the invitation.

Call screening and the phrase "May I tell him or her who is calling" are so common in the business world that few people object to them. Callers who are confident they have something to offer are also confident they will get through your screen.

Some people will object to call screening. Most people have their secretaries put through these difficult callers so that they don't accidentally insult a major client or other VIP. Be sure your secretary knows what to do when a caller won't give his or her name.

If you are unavailable to everyone—if you are in a meeting, out of the office, or entertaining a visitor, for example—have your secretary state this before asking for the name of the caller. Callers appreciate not being screened, and if your secretary offers to pull you out of a meeting after hearing a VIP's name, you have made it clear how important that caller is to you.

Don't give your secretary a script to read. Pat responses can't effectively screen callers. Your goal is to give your secretary the tools and skills needed to handle all types of calls. When call screening is a process, and not just a reading of a script, unusual calls can be screened as efficiently as routine calls.

Taking Messages

A standard "while you were out" pad is sufficient for taking messages—as long as it is complete. If you need special information to return phone calls productively, you can design your own form and have it made into a pad. However, keep in mind that secretaries often have a hard time completing even short message forms. Busy callers don't always have the patience to spell out their names and leave phone numbers, let alone answer other questions.

Ideally every phone message should include:

- the caller's name
- the company name
- telephone number, including the area code

Instruct your secretary to prompt callers for this information if necessary.

Many callers rush through their messages and hang up before the information can be checked. Therefore, have your secretary read back spellings and phone numbers letter by letter and number by number as the caller goes along. It is also helpful to know the nature of the call, but often the message is too complicated to transcribe in a short amount of time. A quick phrase from the caller ("I want to reschedule our lunch") and a few words on the message pad ("Re: rescheduling lunch") can save valuable time for everyone in the long run.

Have your secretary arrange your phone messages in order of importance. This saves you the trouble of picking through them trying to figure out what is important. Telemarketers have found that phone calls are placed more quickly if you don't have to decide which to make first but just dial through a stack of messages.

Also ask your secretary to gather materials pertinent to your messages. If the call concerns a letter, for example, have your secretary retrieve it from your correspondence file and clip it to the message. If customer records will make the call-back more productive, have your secretary retrieve the file containing those records.

Other Rules to Set

Secretaries should always be polite and pleasant on the telephone. Their greeting usually sets a caller's first impression of you and your company. How should your secretary answer your telephone? A variation of your own telephone greeting is best. "Terry Johnson's office. This is Lee Smith." is fine. If your secretary answers calls for the whole department, a greeting stating the department name and the secretary's name is less confusing.

HANDLING RINGING PHONES

Things sometimes get hectic, but phones should never ring off the hook with no one answering them. Few things make a worse impression on a caller than having a call go unanswered during business hours. You should arrange for someone to cover your phone when both you and your secretary are unavailable.

You may also want to set a policy at the department level for ringing phones. "People use customer service to differentiate between companies, and companies need every edge they can get over their competitors," says Leslie Hansen Harps, president of the Customer Service Institute of Silver Spring, Maryland. "Customer service is everyone's business, and whenever the phone rings it's a 'customer.' Even internal calls represent a kind of customer."

The most important thing a manager can do to assure calls are answered promptly, Harps says, is to *set a policy* and put it in writing. The policy should outline tiers of telephone answerers and specify a number of rings after which the phone will be answered by the next tier. Calls can be automatically routed by your telephone system to the next tier after a certain number of rings, or someone in a neighboring office may simply pick up the ringing telephone.

For example, your company policy may state that if a staff member's telephone rings more than four times it will be answered by the departmental secretary. If it is not answered after six rings (because the departmental secretary is not available), it should be answered by the staff member's nearest neighbor. And at a certain point (seven or eight rings), anyone who hears the phone ringing should answer it.

"Answering other people's telephones benefits the team," says Harps. When other staff members answer calls the efficiency of the whole department is improved. "Your staff can't say, 'That's not my call; that's not my job.' Everyone is on the same team," she says.

If you have a private line, don't forget to include it when setting the telephone answering policy for the department. Often your private line isn't automatically routed to another phone if you don't answer it. Since your most important calls may be coming over this line it is especially important that your secretary, assistant, or other staff members know how these calls should be handled.

Harps feels that today's technology leaves no excuse for telephones that are not answered. If, after setting an answering policy, your department's phones are still ringing off the hook, she recommends considering a voice mail system.

HAVING YOUR SECRETARY PLACE CALLS FOR YOU

"It is not unprofessional to have a secretary place a call for you," says Dr. Baker, "but it is unprofessional not to be on the phone within five or six seconds." If you are having a difficult time reaching someone, having your secretary place the call for you can save time. But you must be ready to speak to the person immediately when the call is put through.

Don't keep the person you called waiting. This implies, even if you don't intend it to, that your time is much more valuable than the time of the person you are calling. Getting on the phone promptly shows the consideration necessary for a productive phone conversation.

When you receive a call placed by a secretary, expect to be connected to the caller within five or six seconds. If you refuse to wait at all you come across as unprofessional, says Dr. Baker, but it is up to you to set the limit on how long you will wait. He feels twenty seconds is a reasonable limit to set—but that is a generous limit, and you may find it is too long. Respecting other people's time and being sure your own is respected is one of the keys to greater telephone effectiveness.

CHAPTER 5

HOW TO GET IN TOUCH WITH ANYONE BY TELEPHONE:

*Suggestions on
How to Reach
Your Goals*

Many are stubborn in pursuit of the path they have chosen, few in pursuit of the goal.

—Friedrich Wilhelm Nietzsche

When you make a business call, there is usually a good reason for it. You may want to deliver a message, need information, or hope to buy or sell something. If the person you are calling is difficult to reach, you may get frustrated and lose sight of the reason for your call. When this happens, it may be helpful to focus on the goal of your call. Contacting an individual is merely the means to reaching that goal.

The point of a business call is *rarely simply* to speak with someone. A business call may have a social aspect. For instance, you may call a client to say hello, to ask how things are, or to "touch base." Usually a business call has a *goal*. You may need to deliver a message, need information, or hope to buy or sell something. Reaching an individual is merely the means to reaching that goal.

Before you make any telephone call, you should have a *clear idea* of what you want to accomplish with that call. If you suspect it will be difficult to reach a person or if your calls are not being returned, you must sit down and separate what you *want* to accomplish from what you *need*.

You may want to call up the CEO of a Fortune 500 company, impress him with your sales acumen, and not only sell him millions of dollars' worth of your product, but have your name on his lips for the next two months as the best salesperson in the business.

In reality, if you need to sell a product to a Fortune 500 company you will be stonewalled if you start with the CEO. It is easy to be led off track by pursuing an industry leader or someone with a prestigious title. That is why it is important to keep the *goal* of your phone call in mind. It may be impossible to talk to that person with the prestigious title, but you can often contact someone else who can help you achieve the goal of your call.

In most telephone conversations, both parties have a good idea of "what's in it for me" even if it is never stated. The salesperson for example, wants your order; you want the product. You want the product fixed; the customer service department wants a satisfied customer who will buy again.

Salespeople are trained to think, not about selling a product to a customer, but the product's benefits. They know they don't sell drill bits, they sell holes. When you are trying to reach someone by telephone, you should know what *benefits* your conversation will have for the person you are calling. You may never have to mention the benefit, but if you know what it is, you can use it to persuade a secretary, an assistant, or a supervisor to let you speak to that person.

In some cases, knowing the benefit helps you choose your course of action. Not getting satisfaction from the customer service department? Call your salesperson. The benefits may be hazy to a front-line customer service person who is just trying to get through a shift, but your salesperson knows future commission checks are on the line.

Do not overlook altruism. Most people like to help others. Be sure to let the person you are calling know if your conversation will help you. Of course, this approach loses its effectiveness quickly. Most people will be glad to help you a few times or do a small favor. But if you ask too often, people begin to expect something in return.

THE TECHNIQUE

Once you have defined your goals and know the benefits of your call, there are a few strategies that will help you reach anyone by telephone.

Be Persistent

If the call is important to you and you cannot get through the first time, try again and again. How frequently you should call depends on how urgent the conversation is and if it is more important to you or the person you are calling. If you are calling to give someone information he or she requested, a single phone call is sufficient. Leave the information with a secretary if the person cannot answer your call or leave a message stating that you have the information.

If the call is more important to you, there are some useful rules of thumb to use. If you must speak to someone by the end of the day, call back every few hours. Each time, leave a message explaining the urgency of your call. If you need to speak to someone within a few days or a week, call once a day. Ask what time of day is best to call or if there is one day when the person will be available, and call back at that day and time.

There is a big difference between being persistent and being a pest. The idea is to get across the urgency of your call and your willingness to make the call happen. If you try to harass people into calling you back, you may get the person to call, but he or she will probably be less responsive to what you have to say.

Let's say your personnel department is in charge of placing help wanted advertisements in the newspaper, and you have an opening in your department that needs to be filled immediately. You want to know if personnel has placed the ad. If the deadline for Sunday's paper is several days away, you may want to leave a message every day or so. If the deadline arrives and your call still has not been returned, leave a message every few hours and make it clear there is a deadline to be met. Keep in mind that the other party may be busy also. Don't cry wolf by marking a message urgent when the call can wait.

Be Patient

Don't be discouraged or feel insulted if your call is not promptly returned. If the person has been out of town, your message may be at the bottom of a huge stack. Many people return calls to people they know first, then work their way through the unfamiliar names. When two or three message slips with your name on them pile up, your call may be bumped to the top of the stack.

If your call is not urgent, you should be willing to wait until the person has time to return it. Your reward for waiting may be a relaxed conversation and the full attention of the person. Remember: Be sure that the person you are calling is aware of your deadlines. A relaxed conversation is worth nothing if it comes too late.

Make an Appointment

One way to assure your conversation is both relaxed and prompt is to set up a time for the call ahead of time. It is a good idea to make an appointment or offer to make an appointment for any conversation you expect to last more than ten minutes. If you reach someone who sounds frantic, ask when to call back, even if the call will be a short one. The person will most likely appreciate how considerate you are of his or her time. In other cases, after you greet the person and explain briefly the purpose of your call, say, "I expect this to take twenty minutes. Do you have time to talk now?" If the person says no, ask what day and time you can call back. Give the caller a specific time frame. Ask, "What time today would be better to call you?" or "What day this week is best for you?"

Treat a telephone appointment as you would any other appointment or meeting. Making an appointment also allows the person you are calling to treat the conversation like a meeting. The person has the opportunity to close the door, ask the secretary to hold all calls, and have the materials you need on hand. Take advantage of the time you have to *prepare* and do the same thing. Making a telephone appointment gives you the advantage of talking to someone who has set aside a block of time to speak with you, but it can also make demands on your time.

Be Flexible

If you are trying to speak with someone who is very busy and you ask to make an appointment, the person may ask to make it before or after regular business hours. If the conversation will benefit you more than it will benefit the person you are calling, it is in your best interest to accommodate this request. In fact, if you want to do an end run around a call screening system, try calling very early in the morning, after business hours, or during lunch. Many busy executives answer their own telephones during these times.

You should also be flexible about which person you call. The one you call first may be able to refer you to someone else who can better help you or may ask an assistant or a staff member to handle your call. It is easy to forget the ultimate goal of your conversation when you are in hot pursuit. Don't lose focus. You should be willing to speak to anyone who can help you.

View Secretaries and Assistants as Allies and Treat Them with Respect

If you can't reach a busy executive, ask her secretary who else in the organization can help you. Explain what you need from the conversation. In many cases, secretaries know who can help you accomplish your goal.

The secretary is also in a position to put your message on top of a pile, remind the boss to call you, or report on what a jerk you are. Many people recognize how valuable their own secretaries and assistants are, but some still treat other people's secretaries and assistants as barriers to getting through. You will reap more rewards by treating a secretary as another business associate. Learn his or her name and take the time to say hello when you call. You never know when it will be helpful to have an ally in the office.

Do not overlook secretaries as a valuable source of information. They may be able to tell you when you can expect your call to be returned or other information about the company. Let's say you are looking for a job and are cold calling companies. The company receptionist may be able to tell you:

- if there are any job openings at the company
- if the company is busy and growing, or laying people off
- if the company employs someone with the responsibilities or a job title similar to what you are looking for
- the name of that person's supervisor

When you reach the supervisor's secretary you can ask:

- if the department is planning to expand
- what specific qualifications the supervisor is looking for in a candidate for the open position
- when is the best time to reach the supervisor

By using secretaries as allies and sources of information, you have taken the chill out of your cold call.

BE APPRECIATIVE

We should all say thank you and show our appreciation for the help we get, but few of us do. Was a customer service representative particularly helpful? Call his boss and say so. Was your conversation with the southwestern regional sales director just what you needed to make your presentation a killer? Write her a thank-you note. Even just saying thank you at the end of the conversation paves the way for future successful conversations. If you are the one who shows appreciation, your calls will be returned promptly in the future.

WHEN YOUR CALLS ARE NOT RETURNED

It happens. You left a message, but your call has not been returned, and you don't know why. The first step is to lay out the goal of your conversation, the benefits for the person you are calling, your deadline, and the consequences if the person does not return your call.

This is not the time for threats. You will be resented, or worse, sound silly. But if, for instance, your supplier does not understand that you will go to someone else for your order if you do not hear from him by 4 P.M., by all means spell it out. Leave this last-ditch message on voice mail, with a secretary or fax a note (ask the secretary or receptionist for the fax number).

What if this doesn't work? You have a few options:

Talk to the Boss

See if someone else can answer your question or if the company is simply not interested in what you have to say. Many managers hate to be bothered, so they will quickly direct you to the person who can help you. And once they have done that, you have the extra leverage of having been referred by the boss. A secretary or assistant can also help you find someone else to talk to, but these people's names rarely will open doors—unless they happen to be the boss's secretary or assistant.

Write a Letter

Writing is a slow method, but sometimes letters get through when phone messages get lost. If your message is urgent, send the letter by fax.

Make a Dramatic Statement

Fax a jumbo-sized "While You Were Out" message form with "Bet You Can't Lose This One" across the top, send a letter or a telegram explaining the urgency of your message, or deliver flowers or balloons with your message attached. Just don't overdo it. It is easy to get dramatic in the heat of the moment. Before you make your dramatic statement, ask yourself how it will reflect on you and your company. Will it seem unprofessional or goofy? Will you come across as hysterical? Is it worth it?

Have a Backup or a "Back Door"

Do not tie yourself to one supplier or prospect. If you run into trouble, the easiest thing to do is move on to the next call. Sometimes simple inefficiency or bad business practices are keeping your calls from being returned. You must decide if you still want to do business with that company. Is there someplace else to get the information? Is there someone else at the company who can help you? Keep your ultimate goal in mind and try not to get sidetracked by the pursuit of a single person.

Let's say you want to buy a photocopier. You wonder if it needs to be on its own electrical circuit. The salesperson doesn't know, but he says he will ask one of his technical people to give you a call. A few days pass, and you haven't received a call. You call the salesperson, and he says the technical people haven't called him either. Is there someone else in the company who can help you? You may find out that the service manager can answer your question. Is there another source for this information? The manufacturer? A product brochure? If no one at this company can answer your question, or if they take a long time to reply, you may consider buying a copier from another company that will give you better service.

TAKE A STEP BACK

It can be very frustrating when you cannot reach someone by telephone. If this happens, it is best to take a step back and try to be objective.

Do you have a clear goal? Is the person you are trying to reach the best person to help you reach that goal? Have you asked that person's secretary or assistant if there is someone else who can help you? Have you explained to the person how he or she can benefit from your call?

Sometimes it is best to try another approach. The person may not be getting your messages or just may not respond well by telephone. Change your strategy. Send a message by letter or fax. Call at another time of day (when a busy executive may answer her own calls). Find another contact at the company.

VIPs may take a little longer—they require more motivation to return your calls. But a person is only as important as he or she is to you and your goals. Be persistent, patient, and accommodating and you will increase your chances of reaching your VIP.

CHAPTER 6

SELLING BY TELEPHONE:

*More Effective
Techniques
from the Pros*

One of the best ways to persuade others is with your ears—by listening to them.

—Dean Rusk

Y ou sit down to dinner and the phone rings. "Is this Mr. West? How are you this evening? My name is Pat and I'd like to tell you about our exciting new product. Have you heard of our product? Well, let me tell you a little about it…" And off Pat goes, explaining benefits and features without a pause. When you finally say you are not interested, Pat launches into another speech. At the next pause you say, "I'm sorry, I'm not interested," and hang up. Another perfect example of how not to sell by telephone.

Even if your profession is personnel, accounting, or field sales, you should know the basic techniques of selling over the telephone. Whether you have to convince a department that your recruitment plan is the best one, persuade your auditors that your internal controls are adequate, or set up a meeting with a client, you are selling over the phone. Even non-salespeople do a lot of "selling" by phone.

CONSULTIVE SELLING

After years of experience with old-fashioned, hard-sell salespeople, you may think telephone selling requires a silky voice, a well-rehearsed sales pitch, and a snappy answer for every objection. Actually, it requires none of these things. Skilled salespeople know they are in the business of helping people. The technique they use is called *consultive selling*.

Consultive selling puts an emphasis on what the customer needs and wants. It involves listening more than talking; objections are addressed, not overcome. It focuses on questions. The seller asks a series of questions to find out if and how the seller's product, service, or idea will help the prospect. The questions are probing and open-ended. The salesperson looks for needs and desires that are not being met or that can be met more fully. For most of the process, the salesperson just listens.

PLANNING AHEAD

Consultive selling begins before you even pick up the telephone. According to Art Sobczak, an Omaha, Nebraska-based telephone sales trainer and publisher of the *Telephone Selling Report*, you should do these four things before making any persuasive call:

1. Write down specifically what you need to accomplish in this phone call. What do you want the person you are calling to do at the end of your conversation? What do you want to be doing?
2. Find out as much as possible about the person you are going to call.
3. Plan exactly what you are going to say in the first fifteen to twenty seconds of the phone call.
4. Prepare your questions.

Use this time to tell the person you are calling why he or she should be interested in your call. The person must know the benefit of staying on the telephone with you. In those first few seconds, you must explain

- who you are
- why you are calling

- what is in it for the other party
- why he or she should spend time with you and answer your questions

During this time, become acquainted with the person you are calling; do not present a sales pitch. "Too many people give their presentation and their close before they know anything about the person they are selling to," says Sobczak. "You sell more by asking questions than by making statements."

Since questions, not a sales pitch, are the focus of consultive selling, carefully prepare your list of questions. What do you need to know to persuade the person you are calling to take the course of action you want him or her to take? Do not limit yourself to practical matters. Hopes, dreams, and desires are powerful persuaders. When you have completed your precall planning, you are already ahead of most other people.

Choosing the Right Person

If you are trying to sell to people with a particular job title, such as the "personnel director," do not simply ask to speak to the personnel director when you reach a company. Ask for the name of the person who holds that position, then ask to be transferred.

If a secretary answers the phone, take advantage of the opportunity to learn more about the person you are trying to reach. Ask the secretary what the boss is looking for in your product or service, or ask a question that gives you a better idea of what the person is like. Sobczak has found that a phrase like this works well: "I would like to speak to Ms. Johnson, but first can you tell me…"

Asking Questions

When you reach your party, remember that you have approximately fifteen to twenty seconds to explain who you are and why the party you are calling should be interested in your call. Once you have the person's attention, begin asking questions. "The only way to sell is by asking questions," says Sobczak. "Find out if there is a need, an interest, or an urgency. Find out if this person can make the decision and has the budget needed to buy your product or implement your idea."

Ask amplifying questions as well: "Please explain that." "Can you give a specific example?" "Why do you follow that particular procedure?" "How did you reach that figure?" Sometimes a simple answer is not what it appears to be. Dig deeper. Find out what the person is really saying. If you settle for the pat answer, you will be hampered later on when you try to use the information you have gathered.

There are *recognized* and *unrecognized* needs. If you are lucky your prospects will know what they need. But if they don't recognize their needs, you have to help them. You can do this by asking more questions or making statements that make the needs more apparent to the prospect.

Making the Presentation

The next step, the actual presentation, is easy if you have spent time getting to know your prospects. Because you already know about them, you can focus on the benefits and features that fill their needs. Your presentation can be brief. If your prospects are interested in the bottom line, tell them how your proposed work schedule will save money. If they are interested in safety, show how it will reduce job-related injuries. If you did not know your prospects you would have to give them every detail, hoping to hit on one or two that appeal to them. Since you have already analyzed what appeals to them, you can deliver just the meat of the presentation.

"When I give a seminar, this is the shortest part of my discussion," says Sobczak. "You have found out their wants, needs and desires. There has to be one specific item you can address." Since you know these things, tailor your presentation to address what you have discovered.

Closing the Sale

Even though you are avoiding the hard sell, you must remember to "close"—to ask for the sale or an agreement with your proposal. Every Girl Scout knows she must ask "Would you like to buy some cookies?" It is hard to believe that adults—even professional salespeople—forget or avoid asking for an agreement. Actually, it is very common.

Many salespeople find themselves with a long list of prospects to call back and few sales. This is the sign of a poor closer or a salesperson who is afraid to ask for an agreement.

After getting so involved with your prospect, you may find it awkward to bluntly ask him or her to do what you want. Sobczak recommends saying, "Based on what you've already told me, it sounds as if you already have made up your mind."

If a decision cannot be made immediately, make sure you both know what has to be done next. Every persuasive call should end with both parties taking some action. Have the person send you something by mail—such as a union contract specifying certain work hours, in the case of the work schedule change. If the person you spoke to must get someone else's approval to proceed, make sure he or she is sold first. The prospect is now your salesperson. Ambivalence on the part of this person won't do your cause much good. Your prospects should also know what you will be doing next. Will you mail them further information? Get back to them with the answer to a question?

Answering Objections

Chances are your prospect will not immediately say yes when you close. Instead he or she may have objections. "The best way to answer an objection is to ask more questions, not to fire off a prepared response," says Sobczak.

Luckily, most people hate to say no. Unfortunately, most people will not be specific about their reasons for not agreeing with you.

Respond to objections with "Let's talk about that." For example, a colleague may say he won't back your proposal because of the financial impact on the company. What he may mean is he is afraid your proposal will postpone an expansion of his department. If you fire back a retort explaining the financing of your proposal in general terms, you won't have answered his real objection.

"Talking through objections is a painless way to pull your chair over to the other side of the desk," says Sobczak. "Don't try to overcome objections; instead, answer them. Overcoming an objection implies a winner and a loser—and you don't want that."

THE TRIANGLE APPROACH

Think of persuading or selling as a triangle with the point at the bottom. The width of the triangle is the amount of time you spend on each stage. You need to spend a lot of time before you even make the call. You must know what you need to accomplish and something about the person you are speaking with. You need to plan what you will say in the first few seconds and you must prepare questions to find out more about the person and his or her needs.

When you ask the questions, you primarily will be listening. The question-and-answer stage can take a long time. Once your questions are answered satisfactorily, you can make your presentation: explain to the person why he or she should support your idea or buy your product. This statement can be brief. Focus on the points you know will interest your prospect or co-worker.

And don't forget the brief phrase in which you ask for agreement on the sale. "Will you back me in the meeting?" or "Will you buy the product?" This phrase is the point of the triangle, and the point of your call.

If the person says "no," ask why he or she doesn't agree with you. Don't overcome the person's objections, answer them. Say "Let's talk about that" to get the person to elaborate on his or her response. Again, you are listening more than talking. You are back at the question-and-answer stage.

When you use a consultive selling approach both sides win. Even if you do not persuade your co-worker to back you in this case, you begin a relationship and sow the seeds of future agreements. If the elements needed for both sides to be satisfied do not exist now, things may come together down the road. If you do not change anyone's mind on your first call, do not give up.

A study conducted by the Marketing Department at the University of Notre Dame showed that the average telephone sale was made after five attempts to close the sale. Yet many telephone sellers give up long before that. When you use professional selling techniques that benefit the person you are calling as much as they benefit you, those phone calls are easier to make and are more likely to end in success.

CHAPTER 7 USING TELEPHONE TECHNOLOGY:

*How to Make
Technology Work
for You—
Not Against You*

Many jobs are changing because of technology advances, and a highly competent occupant on any rung of the ladder may become obsolete through failure to move with the times.

—Dr. Laurence J. Peter *(Why Things Go Wrong)*

Telephone technology includes cellular phones, facsimile machines, automated attendants, and a host of other gadgetry. It's a big change from the telephone technology that was common just ten years ago. In the past few years, new telephone technology has become a fixture in the business world—but office policies and business etiquette haven't always kept up. With a little insight and some common sense, you can be the master of this technology. Today's telephone may be more complicated than yesterday's simple dial and receiver, but, used correctly, it is a more powerful tool.

AUTOMATED ATTENDANTS

If you have ever called a company and heard a recorded announcement welcoming you and asking you to press an extension, to press zero for the operator, or to "hold the line and an operator will be with you shortly," you have been greeted by an automated attendant. You probably either love *auto attendants* or hate them—few people sit on the fence for this issue. But even if you hate auto attendants there are a few techniques you can use that will help you get along with them a little better.

OTHER COMPANIES

When you know the extension of the person you are calling you can skip the long instruction and selection menus, the wait for the operator, even the initial greeting. Immediately punch in the extension of the person you are trying to reach as soon as you hear a recorded voice. If you call another company and are greeted by an auto attendant, there is not much you can do if you are not prepared. With so many of these devices around, the best thing to do is to *become an avid collector of people's telephone extensions.*

Get into the habit of always getting a person's extension when you get his or her telephone number. Add extensions to your records: in your phone book, on your Rolodex—and jot them on business cards when you receive them, if an extension isn't printed in. Having telephone extensions turns auto attendants into time-savers; without them they are time-wasters.

If you are calling a specific person but don't know the extension, hit *0* as soon as you hear the recording. This will transfer you immediately to the operator and eliminates having to listen to the entire recorded greeting.

YOUR COMPANY

There is much you can do to make your company's auto attendant work more effectively for you and your callers.

1. Use the auto attendant on "back door" telephone lines—those lines not used by first-time callers or potential customers.
2. Present the auto attendant as a benefit or a valuable service to your employees, frequent customers, and suppliers. Point out that the auto attendant will give them instant access to the party they wish to reach. They will no longer have to wait for a receptionist to pick up the phone and transfer the call.

3. Don't expect an auto attendant to replace personal assistance from a company receptionist or a departmental secretary. If they wish to, callers should always be able to reach a human being.

4. Don't surprise callers with a new automated attendant. Write letters to your contacts explaining the new system and giving them your extension.

5. Keep recorded greetings short.

6. Limit menus to three or fewer options at a time. Too many options will confuse callers.

7. Have new business cards and stationery printed that include your telephone extension in addition to your telephone number.

If you are greeted by an auto attendant, voice mail is sure to follow. Using voice mail effectively is discussed in Chapter 8.

FACSIMILE

While auto attendants are only effective for people familiar with them, facsimile—or fax—is a technology with few enemies. Indeed, the biggest problem with fax machines, it seems, is not having one. There are several things you can do to make your fax more effective:

1. Small type, and certain typefaces, don't transmit clearly. Use the largest type possible on your faxes—it should be at least ten-point type. Dot-matrix printing, for example does *not* fax well. Try to avoid it. Laser printing however does fax well.

   Adobe Systems, a computer graphics company, tested several typefaces and rated the following as the best for faxing in this order: *Palatino; Helvetica; ITC Bookman; New Century School Book; Courier.*

   1. Palatino
   2. Helvetica
   3. ITC Bookman
   4. New Century School Book
   5. Courier

2. A cover sheet adds privacy to your fax message. Letters come in envelopes and phone calls are heard by only one person, but fax messages are there for anyone to read. The cover sheet gives your fax message an "envelope" so its contents can't be easily read by everyone who handles it.

3. Call before or after sending a fax. Many companies have not yet worked the bugs out of their fax distribution system. If the recipient is expecting the fax or knows it has arrived, there is a better chance he or she will actually receive it.

4. Don't believe everything your fax machine says. Some machines have a display or a tone that "confirms" the fax has arrived at the receiving machine. However, this confirmation does not mean your fax has really reached its intended recipient, or that the entire fax has been printed out at the receiving machine. Many things can go wrong, even if you get a confirmation. If it is important, check to make sure the fax has arrived.

5. Faxes printed on thermal paper are delicate. Never put a fax on a heater, radiator, or in direct sunlight. Thermal paper reacts to the heat of the fax machine typehead by turning black. It will do the same on your windowsill, blacking out all that was printed there.

   Faxes printed on high-quality thermal paper last about five years if they are kept away from heat and direct light. Cheap fax paper fades more quickly—in a few years, or even a few months. If you need a permanent copy of the fax—for legal reasons or for storing the fax in a permanent file—or if you are not sure of the quality of your paper, make a photocopy.

6. The big advantage fax messages have over telephone messages is that they don't necessarily interrupt your work. If someone is going to call you back with a quick confirmation, approval, or brief message, ask him or her to fax it to you instead of calling. You can

handle the message when it's most convenient for you, not whenever the call happens to come in. (See sample fax cover sheets as follows.)

TO _____

CO. _____

FAX # _____

FROM _____

CO. _____

FAX # _____

PAGES _____

Canon
FAX

A post-it-note, like this one, with all the important fax information in a small space, is really all you need to send a fax.

FACSIMILE COVER SHEET

[YOUR COMPANY NAME OR LOGO]

TO: _____

COMPANY: _____

FAX NUMBER: _____

FROM: _____

COMPANY: _____

FAX NUMBER: _____

TELEPHONE NUMBER: _____

This fax has _____ pages, including this cover sheet.

The idea behind a fax cover sheet is that the person you send the fax to should have enough information to:

- determine if he or she has received all the pages sent;
- know who to contact if he or she has not received the complete transmission;
- reply to your fax by fax immediately; and
- call you immediately by telephone to acknowledge receipt of the fax or ask more questions.

FAX BOARDS

If you work at a PC and find yourself printing letters and then faxing them, you may want to consider using a facsimile board. A fax board slides into one of the empty slots in your PC (IBM and compatible microcomputer). It lets you convert a text (or graphics) file in your computer and fax it to another fax machine or fax board-equipped computer.

Fax boards cost from several hundred to several thousand dollars. They can be very simple or quite sophisticated. In most cases, a fax board will cost much less than a fax machine with the same features.

Fax boards can save on paper if you fax many letters or memos, but mostly they save you time. If you have to find a fax machine in another department or on another floor—or if you have to wait on line to use the company fax machine—a fax board can give you a significant time savings.

Fax boards are also convenient if you often send the same fax message to many people. The fax board can be programmed to send the faxes automatically—even after business hours to save on phone costs.

All fax boards must convert your computer files into faxable form before they can be sent. This process takes about as long as printing the document. Some fax boards convert more quickly than others, just as some printers print more quickly than others.

Fax boards are much more suited to sending faxes than receiving them. Most fax boards will let you enlarge or reduce the size of the fax on your computer screen. They will even let you turn the fax top-to-bottom in case it was sent upside down. (This is quite common. You don't notice it on a regular fax machine.) In spite of these features, faxes are much more legible on paper. Therefore you may find yourself printing the faxes you receive.

CELLULAR TELEPHONES

Since you pay for both incoming and outgoing calls on your cellular telephone it is important that you control the calls. Give out the number of your cellular phone sparingly, and make it clear it is to be used only for urgent calls.

Compared to your cellular phone bill, a pager (or beeper) with an LCD display is relatively inexpensive. Have callers dial your beeper number instead of your cellular phone. When you recognize the phone number of someone you wish to speak to immediately, you can call him or her back on your cellular phone (since you pay the same amount whether you make or receive a call). The pager will store other numbers so that you can return them later on a regular (less expensive) telephone.

Using a pager will also assure that you don't miss calls when the power on your phone runs low. This is especially important if you use a portable or transportable cellular phone that doesn't draw power from your car battery. Even if the power is low you can still make calls, so you may not know there is a problem. But you won't be able to receive calls—callers will hear a ringing, but your phone won't ring. With a pager, you will get all your calls.

When you make a business call on your cellular phone, "be sure to let it slip that you are calling from your car," says Stuart F. Crump Jr., publisher of *Cellular Sales and Marketing* and *The Portable Office* newsletters. "Not to impress them, but to let them know this is a business call. Cellular calls still give the impression that long distance phone calls used to convey: that this is an important call. You will find you are on the phone a much shorter time."

HEADSETS

Do you end the day with a sore neck? sore shoulders? Do your ears burn? Is your arm cramped? All of these problems are symptoms of having spent too much time on the phone. You probably can't solve these problems by cutting down on phone time, but you can take a cue from telephone operators and telemarketers and use a headset. For years headsets were regarded as tools for receptionists. Because anyone wearing a headset was viewed as support staff, managers were reluctant to wear them.

Headset manufacturers are aware of this feeling. So they have come out with a new line of "executive headsets" with an emphasis on personal choice and appearance. More and more managers are using the new style headsets, but you still have to expect some surprised looks when someone walks into your office when you are wearing one. Is it worth it?

Not only does a headset cut down on those phone-related aches and pains, it helps you get more work done if you need two hands to take notes, access a computer, or search through files while on the phone. A study performed by research firm H.B. Maynard & Company for Plantronics (a headset manufacturer) showed that salespeople, travel agents, technical field sales support people, and stockbrokers were 43 percent more productive when they used a headset, depending on how fast their computers were and how fast they typed.

CONTROLLING PHONE COSTS

The most important thing to do to control recurring telephone costs is to choose the correct long distance service for your company's usage. That is, not just the best long distance company, but the best service or plan the company offers. There is no easy way out of making this decision. In some large companies there is an employee whose only job is to constantly evaluate the company's phone usage and find the best long distance service for that usage pattern.

Common Cost-Cutting Techniques

In most companies the most effective telephone cost-cutting techniques (choosing a long distance service, auditing equipment charges from your local telephone company) probably will be the responsibility of the tele-communications department, purchasing department, or office manager. But there are a few things you can do within your own department to cut down on telephone costs:

- Make sure employees know that WATS (Wide Area Telephone Service) lines are not free. There are persistent rumors about this in some companies, but it is not true. Companies pay for all WATS calls.
- Make sure employees know that someone always pays for 800 number calls. This is important if your company has more than one location. Employees may call between locations on the company's 800 numbers thinking those calls are free. In some cases your company may be paying more for the 800 call than they would for a call on their regular telephone number. Make sure employees use the least expensive method of calling between company locations whether it's a tie-line, a regular telephone number, or an 800 number.
- Set a personal calls policy. Many managers feel a policy of no personal calls at all is too restrictive. You probably will want to restrict international calls because they can be quite expensive. Domestic long distance calls are another story. In many cases a long distance call costs no more than a local call. Time wasted on personal calls should be the issue, rather than the cost of the calls themselves. Whatever policy you set, be sure it is explained clearly when an employee joins your department.

Today's telephone technology can make you a more effective telephone communicator, or it can stand in your way. In most cases, the difference is just a little effort on your part. With the help of these tips, technology can create entirely new opportunities for you.

CHAPTER 8

USING VOICE MAIL:

*A Help
or a Hindrance
to Your
Telephone
Effectiveness?*

Perhaps the most important thing that has come out of my life is the discovery that if you prepare yourself...you will be able to grasp opportunity....
Without preparation you cannot do it.

—Eleanor Roosevelt

At the Bertelsmann Music Group (BMG), a prerecorded music and video distributor, regional manager Mike Tawa uses voice mail to take the hassle out of daily new-release reports. The company handles forty to fifty new titles each month. The sales figures on those titles are so important that daily reports are generated to track them. Salespeople call in to a voice mailbox at the end of each day with the figures on the new releases they have sold. The next morning, a sales assistant listens to the messages and enters the figures into a computer program. In no time, the company has the new-release information it needs.

LEAVING VOICE MAIL MESSAGES

Used correctly, voice mail is a tool to enhance your personal effectiveness and your company's productivity. When it comes to leaving voice mail messages, your motto should be "Be Prepared." We have already seen that a good number of business telephone calls won't reach their intended parties. You may have also suspected that a detailed message is more than a busy receptionist can handle. That is where voice mail comes in.

Most voice mail systems let you record a message of any length. Even the ones that put a limit on the length of the message often give you a minute or more. That is long enough for even the most detailed message. Take advantage of it.

Some people, even those who are comfortable with home answering machines, still get steamed when they encounter voice mail. After a few bad experiences with people hiding behind their voice mail, anyone can sour on the concept. People who hide behind voice mail let the machine answer their calls even if they are in the office and not busy. Then they don't return the calls.

The thing to remember about voice mail is that it is not the machine that is keeping you from the person you want to speak to—not if the company is using the system correctly. What voice mail *is* keeping you from is a harried secretary or receptionist who keeps putting you on hold after taking your name and phone number and who hangs up on you before you can leave a message.

Research done by the voice mail industry shows that 50 percent of all phone calls are "one way." One person needs to deliver information to another. With voice mail you don't have to wait until the person calls you back—if you are prepared. When calling to deliver *one-way information,* be ready to leave a complete and coherent message on voice mail. The voice mail system is secure enough for even confidential messages. Voice mail systems require users to enter their mailbox address and a password before they can retrieve their messages.

For people who do business nationwide, voice mail has an added benefit: you do not have to wait until office hours to "speak" to people outside your time zone. If you have a brainstorm at 6 P.M. in California, you can leave a message for someone in New York (even though it is 9 P.M. there) and know that it will be received first thing in the morning.

All is not lost if your phone call is a little more complicated. How many times has this happened to you? You call the shipping department for information on the status of an order. The person you need to speak to is in a meeting, so the department secretary takes a message. Hours later your call is returned. The first question your shipping person asks is, "What is it you wanted?" And, of course, she will have to get back to you later for the ship date on that order.

Voice mail makes things much easier if both parties know what they are doing. Instead of just leaving a message to call you back, leave a message detailing the information the shipping department needs to track the order. You do not have to worry about giving too much detail. Most voice mail systems let the recipient rewind and fast-forward messages much like a tape recorder. (Just remember to speak slowly and clearly—voice mail still cannot fix a garbled message.) With the detail you provide, the person should be able to return your call with an answer to your question, or to mail you the brochure, catalog, or information you requested if you leave your address.

Encountering voice mail is probably most frustrating for salespeople. What can you do to get through to someone who will not return your voice mail messages? One good idea comes from Ken Leebow, president of Voice Information Processing, a voice mail company, located in Marietta, Georgia.

"Don't be discouraged when voice mail keeps you from talking to your prospect," says Leebow. "Use the voice mail system to leave a thirty-second commercial about your product or service. Write a script so voice mail doesn't catch you by surprise. And don't give up after one phone call. Call again in a week and leave another thirty-second commercial."

The final thing to remember about voice mail messages is to always leave your telephone number. Always. One of the big advantages to voice mail is that users do not have to be in the office to retrieve their voice mail messages. They do not even have to call during business hours. When the person you called listens to your message, he or she may not have access to a Rolodex, office files, or industry directory. Even if you think the person knows your phone number, do not take a chance. Leave your number and allow the person to get back to you right away.

YOUR OUTGOING MESSAGE

Most people use their office voice mail just as they use their home answering machine. They record a single, all-purpose message and leave it on for months. At home there are two good reasons for vague answering machine messages: security and privacy. You wouldn't put a message on your answering machine that said, "We will be on vacation for two weeks." It would be an invitation to rob your home. And there is just no reason to tell people "We went to the movies and expect to be back at 11:30."

These factors do not hold in business. Unless you work alone, there is no security risk in telling callers you are out of the office for three days. You may not want to tell every caller you are at a meeting and expect to return to your desk at 2:30, but at least let your callers know you plan to return phone calls around three o'clock that afternoon.

Your voice mail greeting must be specific and timely.

Most voice mail manufacturers recommend that a human being answer all telephone calls and transfer callers to a voice mailbox only with their approval and only when they want to leave a message. While this is the ideal use for voice mail—as a message-taker only—not all companies choose to use it this way. If your company is using voice mail to reduce support staff, you may be forced to use voice mail to answer your calls when you are not at your desk.

When human beings answer your telephone calls, whether they are secretaries, receptionists, or co-workers, they tell your caller if you are out of the office for the day or if you have just stepped away from your desk. They route urgent calls to someone else who might be able to help, and they make sure the caller leaves information, such as account names, that you need to get back to the caller with an answer. Use voice mail to perform these same functions.

With a voice mail system answering your telephone, you have to plan for many factors in your greeting—you can't count on human intelligence (other than your own) to help your callers.

START WITH THE BASICS

All callers need to know your name and the name of your department. Don't forget to include these two important facts at the start of your voice mail message. Voice mail callers also need to know how to get back to the receptionist if their call has been misdirected.

TELL CALLERS WHEN TO EXPECT A RETURN CALL

The voice mail nightmare: the president of your company calls with a quick question on one of your projects. Your voice mail message says, as it always does, "I'm not at my desk right now, but leave a message and I'll get right back to you." You are on vacation for the week, but your boss does not know that. As he leaves message after message he thinks less and less of you.

Change your message before you go on vacation, take a business trip, or leave the office for the day. If you are worried that callers will think less of you for taking a vacation, just say you are out of the office—but let them know when you will be back.

Change your message too, before you go into a marathon meeting. Again, you do not have to say where you are if that makes you uncomfortable. Just let callers know when they can expect their calls returned. Many managers go from one meeting to another without much time in between to return calls. You may not be able to be specific about your schedule, but let your callers know why you are not there to answer their calls: "I will be in and out of meetings all day."

ASK CALLERS WHEN THEY NEED AN ANSWER

Knowing when a reply is needed helps you prioritize your call-backs. Delegate return calls to a member of your staff who can handle them. Most voice mail systems let you forward a voice mail message to someone else on the system and attach comments to the message. The process is as simple as pressing a few buttons on your telephone. If this feature wasn't part of your voice mail basic training, look through your user's guide or ask the system administrator.

TELL CALLERS HOW TO REACH SOMEONE ELSE WHO CAN HELP IF IT'S URGENT

One of the reasons people hate voice mail is its lack of options. You need to reach someone and it is urgent, but you have only two choices: leave a message or hang up. It doesn't have to be that way. If your voice mail system lets callers dial another extension from your greeting (and all decent systems do), let your callers know who can help them when you are not available.

Some systems let you designate a "personal assistant." When the caller hits 0 during your greeting, the call goes to the department secretary or your assistant instead of the company switchboard. Even if your system does not have this feature, ask callers to "dial 327 and speak to my assistant Pat if you need help immediately." Designate different people for different questions so callers get to the person who can best help them. Have them talk to Pat to change an order and Terry to inquire about a shipping date.

Include information on how you can be reached in case of emergency or if you are out of the office. Some systems call you at a telephone number you program to deliver a message when the caller marks his or her call as urgent. This telephone number can be your beeper, your home phone number or the regional office you are visit-ing that day. If your company's voice mail system does not offer this feature, in your greeting you can leave your beeper number or a phone number where you can be reached in case of emergency.

TELL CALLERS WHAT INFORMATION YOU NEED FROM THEM IN ORDER TO ANSWER THEIR QUESTION

There are certain questions your callers frequently ask. And there is certain information you need to answer those questions. Do you need to know which version of a client contract they are referring to? Does your com-pany operate on a fiscal year or a calendar year? Make sure your greeting asks specifically for any information you can not proceed without. The idea is to avoid hav-ing to call back just to get the information you need to answer a question. You want to call back with the an-swer.

Include the answers to commonly asked questions during your greeting, and you may be able to save the return phone call altogether. "The department meeting is at four o'clock today in the conference room." "Sales reports are due on the twentieth of the month." But have pity on other callers who have to listen to the whole greeting before they can leave a message. Keep the greeting brief. If a longer message would be help-ful, direct callers to another mailbox where they can get all the details on the meeting or report.

CHANGE YOUR MESSAGE AS CIRCUMSTANCES WARRANT

Many voice mail greetings invite callers to press zero to reach an operator. But after business hours, when they press zero, no one will answer. Don't tell callers they can reach an operator if they can't. Change the message when the operator goes home for the day.

Don't forget to change your message when you get out of a meeting or return from your vacation. Out-of-date greetings make a bad impression. And while humor has its place—on your home answering machine—your office voice mail message should reflect the professional image your company and department want to convey.

ADVANCED VOICE MAIL FEATURES

There are two voice mail features that are not available on every system but are helpful when they are available. One of these is a voice mail *bulletin board* or "audiotext." Some voice mail systems have a built-in bulletin board feature. Others allow you to take unused voice mailboxes and create your own bulletin board, but your system must be large enough.

Voice mail bulletin boards are used to let callers help themselves to frequently requested information. The initial greeting might ask callers to press 1 for directions to your headquarters, press 2 for the specifications for your latest request for proposal, and press 3 for information on overseas shipping.

The uses for voice mail bulletin boards are limited only by your imagination and the number of mailboxes available in the system. The Super Bowl Host Committee for Super Bowl XXIII in Miami set up a "Super Bowl Hotline" to help Super Bowl guests. Callers to the hotline were offered a choice of several messages including directions to Joe Robbie Stadium from seven nearby communities, typical winter rates for hotels and rental cars, and parking information.

Another advanced feature, *group messaging*, lets you send a single voice mail message to many people inside your company. It saves time by letting you talk instead of write. And it helps you reach employees such as sales-people who are all over the country but call the home office for their messages.

When these sophisticated features are put together voice mail becomes a powerful business tool. Miami-based Labatt Food Service, which supplies condiments and meats to restaurants, hotels, schools, and health care facilities, uses a voice mail system for quick changes in orders. A list of out-of-stock items is broadcast to salespeople each day at 7 P.M. People call into a voice mailbox with substitutions for those items by 9 P.M. Trucks are loaded that night, and the orders, complete with substitutions, are delivered the next morning.

Voice mail is still considered a new and intimidating technology by many. But for those who learn to use it well, the rewards include not only convenience and timesavings, but a new level of telephone effectiveness.

CHAPTER 9

TELECONFERENCING:

*The Next Best Thing
to Being There*

Focus on the people, not on the technology.

—Charlotte Purvis

eleconferencing may seem exotic, but it is not the sole domain of Fortune 500 companies with acoustic conference rooms and fancy equipment. If you have ever used the conference feature of your office telephone to connect a caller with another department and stayed on the line to mediate, you have participated in a teleconference. GAB lines (Group Access Bridge lines), also known as party lines, are really just teleconferences with a steamy agenda.

Teleconferencing includes audioconferencing— voice-only conferences using telephones, speakerphones or microphones and speakers—and videoconferencing, sight and sound conferencing requiring special video equipment and telephone lines. It also includes audio-graphic conferencing (audio conferences enhanced with graphics transmitted by fax or another method) and computer conferences.

TECHNICAL LIMITATIONS

A teleconference is not just a meeting with no visuals. The technology that lets you "meet" with people from around the country or around the world without traveling from your desk also limits those meetings so they are different from face-to-face meetings or telephone calls. Do you attend meetings where everyone talks at once? That can't happen in a teleconference. Do you have a co-worker who is always interrupting at meetings? He or she could easily turn a teleconference into a disaster.

On the simplest level, you must be aware of the conferencing limitations of your office telephone system. You must know how many outside parties and inside lines you can put on a conference. It is not enough to know what the limits are as defined by the user's manual. Phone systems usually do not add amplification to conference calls. This means it quickly becomes difficult to hear what anyone is saying. If your company frequently conducts large conferences by telephone, look into purchasing a teleconferencing bridge—a piece of hardware that is more sophisticated than the conferencing feature available from your phone system—or consider using a teleconferencing service.

Audio technology gets better every day, but there are certain limitations that are expected, especially if you are not using state-of-the-art equipment. First, a teleconference is not a three-way or a ten-way conversation. Only one person can speak at a time. In many systems if one person interrupts another, she seizes the line and no one is able to hear what the first person is saying. Even a loud noise, like a door slamming or a notebook dropping, can cause the system to switch to "listening" to someone other than the person who is speaking.

As the switching on teleconferencing systems gets faster, these systems get closer to sounding like a telephone conversation—where two people can talk at the same time and both hear everything the other person says. To test how quickly a teleconference system switches between speakers, have a person at the other end of the line count to ten with you at a rate you set. How many numbers do you hear? On many systems, whoever spoke first or loudest is the only one heard.

Slow switching between speakers also causes another problem, *clipping*. The teleconferencing system monitors all the lines and gives control to the line with the most noise on it. If someone on another line speaks, it switches control to that line. But listening, recognizing, and switching take a split second, and in that split second a syllable or part of a syllable can be clipped off.

Our expectations of audio teleconferencing are based on the telephone, and our expectations of videoconferencing are based on television. People are disappointed with videoconferencing, warns Steven Hanrahan, a consultant with the Preferred Communications Company of Madison, Wisconsin, because in most cases "it doesn't look like the TV you see at home."

Televisionlike quality is possible, but it requires high-powered telecommunications links that are not only expensive but must be specially installed, door to door, between the sites. In most cases this high quality videoconferencing service is available only between two or more sites designed only for this purpose. It may require traveling across town to the site of a videoconferencing service.

In most cases the quality of the videoconference is reduced so it can be transmitted over more readily available telecommunications links. Even these links are a lot more sophisticated than a regular telephone line. The motion on these transmissions may appear jerky, and you will notice a delay of several seconds between the time you say something and the person at the other end acknowledges.

Another videoconferencing option is a series of still images that are sent as quickly as a few seconds apart. The result is similar to looking at a slide show of still photographs taken with an auto-wind camera.

TELECONFERENCING: BUILDING ON MEETING SKILLS

The experts agree: poor meeting skills are magnified during a teleconference. Things you can get away with in a face-to-face meeting stop a teleconference cold. The first step toward an effective teleconference is to polish your meeting skills.

An agenda is a must for a teleconference. Ideally, the agenda should be prepared well in advance of the teleconference, and a copy sent to all participants. If there is no time to set an agenda before the teleconference, spend the beginning of the meeting developing one. Other materials (charts, diagrams, maps) should also be sent ahead of time to all the participants. These visual aids help focus the participants' attention. They are especially important in long meetings.

Charlotte Purvis, a teleconferencing consultant for Darome Inc., a leading teleconferencing company based in Chicago, suggests preparing and sending ahead of time 25 percent more visual material for an audio-only conference than you would in a face-to-face meeting. In a face-to-face meeting, visuals enhance the message. In a teleconference, they must substitute for your presence.

"Face-to-face meetings are more spontaneous," says Purvis. "You can draw on a chalkboard. For a teleconference you want to think ahead of everything participants would get if you were on site."

For a teleconference that will last more than an hour, Purvis recommends that you include biographical sketches and photographs of the speakers. She has found that people interact more and listen better during a teleconference when they can associate a face with the voice. If the participants have never met in person, a photograph helps bridge the gap.

Of course, in a face-to-face meeting you rely on visuals for more than charts and graphs and knowing what the speaker looks like. Eye contact lets you know if participants are paying attention, if they understand what is being said, and if they wish to ask a question. In a teleconference, accommodations must be made for the lack of visual feedback. You must ask for feedback and listen for it. No teleconference should go more than ten minutes without some kind of shift, warns Purvis. Use a shift between speakers or topics to ask for feedback. Keep a list of the names of the participants in front of you as a visual cue—to replace looking at the faces of people sitting around a conference table.

The technical limitations of teleconferencing change the rules considerably. The way Purvis sees it, the new rules make teleconferencing more polite than a regular meeting. Because different types of teleconferencing equipment have different limitations, the protocol for the teleconference is set by the leader or a moderator who is familiar with the system. The basic limitations of teleconferencing make the following rules necessary:

- One person speaks at a time. Wait for the speaker to finish before you start to talk.
- Identify yourself when you speak.
- Address questions to specific individuals.
- The leader must be sure no one person overwhelms the discussion.

When you participate in a face-to-face conference, you walk into a room, someone closes the door, and you are pretty sure you will not be disturbed until the meeting is over. When you participate in a teleconference, it is up to you to stop disruptions. Before the meeting starts, close the door of your office, and use the "do not disturb" feature on your phone, or tell your assistant or secretary to hold your calls. If the teleconference will be a long one, use the speaker on your telephone or borrow a speakerphone. A headset will also prevent the discomfort that comes with a long telephone call. Purvis suggests calling into the conference three to four minutes before the start of the meeting.

VIDEOCONFERENCING: PREPARING FOR THE CAMERA

As far as your appearance is concerned, preparing for a videoconference is the same as preparing for a television appearance. For example, wearing white may give you a washed-out look. Women should be careful of makeup spots. Glasses don't come across well. Appearing in a videoconference does not make you look like a television star. In fact, you will probably look worse than you do in person.

"You are not going to enhance your image with video," warns Thomas B. Cross, a Boulder, Colorado-based telecommunications consultant specializing in videoconferencing. "The camera puts twenty pounds on you," he says. Cross recommends focusing the video camera on documents, a product demonstration or other visuals during the conference—and keeping it off the participants. Few people feel good about their video image, he says, and knowing they will appear on camera only leads them to avoid videoconferences.

A videoconferencing system is a big investment. If your company has its own system, training or orientation should be available from the videoconferencing staff, the telecommunications department, or the training staff. If your company rents a teleconferencing room from an outside company, that company should be able to provide experts to train you in the particulars of videoconferencing.

Cross says still-frame video is totally overlooked but is effective at adding visuals even on an impromptu basis. He also advocates audio-graphic conferences. An audio-graphic conference pairs an audio teleconference with graphics transmitted by fax during the conference.

WHEN TO TELECONFERENCE

Teleconferences cannot replace face-to-face meetings. Meetings have many functions, and often distributing information or getting input from many people is just a small part of their purpose. A meeting that serves in part to build comraderie or team spirit would not work well as a teleconference. Teleconferencing is also not appropriate when sensitive issues need to be discussed or when delicate negotiations must be made.

Teleconferences work best when all the participants know each other well. Like a telephone call between old friends, the better you know each other the less you rely on visual cues to understand what is being said. Many companies count on teleconferencing to save money on travel costs. At the same time, the costs of a harmful teleconference are more than the travel costs of an effective meeting.

A teleconference is appropriate:

- to replace repetitive calls such as a sales manager's identical calls to all the members of the sales staff
- when it gives people the benefit of hearing other people's questions
- when it takes the place of a routine or regularly scheduled meeting
- when something is too urgent for mail—even overnight mail
- when people complain of being burned out from traveling
- when people feel isolated because everyone is traveling so much they can't keep in touch
- to set the agenda before a big meeting
- to follow up and get feedback after a big meeting

Sandoz Pharmaceutical Corporation has found an innovative use for teleconferencing. Their Interactive Communications Department, headed by Bob del Vecchio, provides audio and videoconferencing for Sandoz Pharmaceutical's health education programs. These programs provide continuing education for physicians and other health professionals. Sandoz links experts on specific disease groups and other subjects with health professionals across the country—even overseas.

The audio conferencing program includes prerecorded video tapes, slides, and printed materials sent to the location beforehand. Teleconferencing equipment is set up when there is a group of two or more in one location. Mr. del Vecchio stresses that the company uses teleconferencing not so much to save money on traveling but to save time for busy health professionals and even busier medical experts.

Sandoz has expanded its health education programs to include the public. Patients with long-term diseases participate in conferences to keep up to date with medical advances related to their disease. Sandoz also provides a health forum on a number of small radio stations around the country. People call in to an 800 number and have their questions answered by health experts.

Sandoz does not try to promote company products in these programs but uses them to convey concern and involvement in the treatment of specific diseases and a dedication to helping health professionals keep up on the latest medical advances. Teleconferencing has proved so successful in these programs that the firm shortly plans to introduce teleconferencing for internal training.

WHEN YOU ARE THE CONFERENCE LEADER

If you are going to moderate a teleconference and you have never participated in one before, arrange to participate in one. If your company uses its own equipment in-house, this may mean sitting in on a conference run by a co-worker. If your company uses a teleconferencing service, contact the service company and ask to sit in on a demonstration meeting.

Even if you have participated in teleconferences before, as a first-time leader you should call your service company or vendor. The company can provide you with a list of features and services. There are so many features available, chances are the one that will help your conference run smoothly is waiting for you. Talk to someone in the reservations department and tell him or her the goal of your meeting. This person will be able to tell you which features and services will help you meet those goals.

Once you are comfortable with the teleconferencing system you will use, schedule the meeting with your conference company or reserve time on the company system. Next, notify the participants and distribute materials to them. If your company image is on the line, for example, at a press conference or stockholders' meeting, have a rehearsal for both the people and the technology.

With a feeling for how a teleconference is similar to a face-to-face meeting and a knowledge of how the technology limits it, you will be able to run a teleconference that is both successful and effective.

The telephone is your most powerful business tool. Not only does it bring the world right to your desk, it lets you talk back to it. The typical business telephone call is brief, but you should not judge its importance by its length. It is through telephone calls that we build relationships, forge alliances, and sell products and services.

Using the telephone effectively means planning your telephone calls before you make them, taking notes on each call, and eliminating telephone tag by leaving messages that specifically state when you will be available to receive calls or finding out the best time to call back.

By using the techniques in this book you will view the new telephone technologies such as voice mail, automated attendants, and teleconferencing as tools for telephone effectiveness instead of roadblocks.

Now that you have added business telephone skills to the social telephone skills you have had for years, you will find the telephone no longer seems to be an interruption to important tasks. It has become a means to accomplish those tasks more effectively.

INFORMATION BY TELEPHONE:

Sample Telephone Manual, International Calling, Time Zone Tables, International Country and City Codes, Useful Telephone Numbers

TELEPHONE NUMBERS FOR MORE INFORMATION

The following manufacturers, vendors, and consultants can give you further information on the subjects listed here. These company listings are not a recommendation or endorsement of the companies' products or services.

Automated Attendants

Audiocom
800-272-0555
305-825-4653

Automation Electronics
415-828-2880

Dytel
708-519-9850

Granite Telecom
603-644-5500

Viking Electronics
715-386-8861

(Also, see Voice Mail)

Customer Service By Telephone

CalTel
818-548-2400

Customer Service Institute and
Customer Service Newsletter
301-585-0730
800-726-5274

Inbound/Outbound Magazine
800-LIBRARY
212-691-8215

International Customer Service Association
312-321-6800

Service Edge Newsletter
800-328-4329
612-333-0471

Telephone Doctor
800-882-9911
314-291-1012

Facsimile Machines

Canon
516-488-6700

Fremont Communications
415-438-5000

Murata
214-403-3300

Pitney Bowes
203-356-5000

Ricoh
201-882-2000

Sharp
800-BE-SHARP
201-529-8200

Toshiba
714-583-3000

Headsets

ACS
408-438-3883
800-538-0742

CommuniTech
708-439-4333

Hello Direct
408-972-1990
800-444-3556

Plantronics
408-426-5868
800-544-4660

Selling By Telephone

Business By Telephone
Telesales Tips Line:
402-896-8477
Telephone Selling Report Newsletter:
402-895-9399

Inbound/Outbound Magazine
212-691-8215
800-LIBRARY

Teleconferencing

AT&T Alliance
800-544-6363

Darome
800-DAROME-1

Sprint Meeting Channel
800-669-1235

Telephone System Training

CalTel
818-548-2400

Telephone Systems

AT&T
800-247-1212

Executone
602-998-2200

Fujitsu
602-921-5900

Mitel
407-994-8500

NEC
516-753-7000

Northern Telecom
214-437-8000

Rolm
203-849-6000
800-926-7656

Siemens
407-994-8800
800-TEL-PLUS

Teleconnect Magazine
800-LIBRARY
212-691-8215

TIE
203-888-8000

Voice Mail

AT&T
908-658-6000

Centigram
408-942-3500

Digital Sound
805-566-2000

Octel
408-942-6500

Rolm
203-849-6000
800-926-7656

Tigon
800-962-2330

VMX
408-441-1144
800-284-4VMX

Here is a list of some of the business 900 numbers available:

Computers

Help with DOS and other MicroSoft software. $2 per minute, first minute free: 900-896-9000

Help with Novell NetWare networking software. $2.99 per minute: 900-PRO-HELP

Legal

For legal advice via telephone from a company called Tele-Lawyer. $3 per minute: 900-INFO-LAW

Stocks

USA Today Money Hotline. Includes stock quotes from the NYSE, AMEX, and NASDAQ. 95¢ a minute: 900-454-3000

JournalPhone. Stock and bond market information, financial and commodity futures news, sports and traveller's weather. 85¢ for the first minute and 75¢ each additional minute: 900-JOURNAL (These are just two of many stock information services.)

Tax

H&R Block's Tax Hotline. $2 for the first minute and $1 each additional minute: 900-226-1444
IRS tax forms faxed to you. $2 for the first minute: 900-860-1040

Travel

American Express weather. 75¢ per minute: 900-WEATHER.
USA Today weather. 75¢ for the first minute and 50¢ for each additional minute: 900-370-USAT

WeatherTrak. 75¢ for the first minute and 50¢ for each additional minute: 900-370-8725 (900-575-8725 in Texas)

Wake-up

For an automated wake-up call. 95¢ per minute. Calls average 2 minutes: 900-773-WAKE (900-773-9253)

Setting Up a Number

If you want information about setting up a 900 number, there are two numbers to choose from. 900-USA-INFO costs $12 per call. 900-370-CASH charges $1 a minute.

SAMPLE TELEPHONE MANUAL

Here's a sample manual you can use to create your own company or departmental telephone guide. All telephone systems work differently, so your company's telephone system probably will be very different from the one described here.

This sample was put together with the help of Lori Korn of CalTel Communications, a telecommunications training and consulting firm. She says, "The telephone user guide should be customized to reflect the company's applications and system programming. Often the guide provided by the manufacturer or vendor has many features or applications that are not appropriate. Or the guide may be incomplete. A dial guide (directory) should also be included. Large companies should also include dial guides for their other offices and a network map, if appropriate."

Policies and Procedures

Trouble Calls

If you are having problems with your telephone: static, low volume, and so on, please call the telecommunications department. We will call the proper repair service. We keep a trouble log of the type and number of trouble calls and the type of telephone so that we can address persistent problems.

In case the telephone system is out of service, please use the red "Hot Line" telephones that are in strategic locations throughout the buildings served by our telephone system.

Personal Calls

Personal calls may be placed in case of emergency, medical purposes, or family care. All toll calls and long distance calls must be reimbursed. Calls must be made at a time that will not interfere with company business, and must have approval of the supervisor.

It is the responsibility of the supervisor to monitor telephone calls and notify each employee monthly of the amount due for provided calls.

911 Emergency Service

In the event of an emergency, you may need to dial 911 to reach the fire department, police department, or paramedics. When reporting an emergency by dialing 911 from your telephone at home, your telephone number and address are displayed automatically on a viewing screen at the 911 call center.

However, when you dial 911 from a telephone on our company telephone system, you must state your location to the 911 operator. The address on the viewing screen is the location where the local telephone lines enter our telephone system—and not the actual building the call is made from.

Your Telephone Set

This user guide provides instructions on the use of your telephone set features designed to make your telephone use easier and more productive.

The telephone has been designed to provide push button access to a host of features. The features on your set have been selected to match your needs based on a survey by the company's telecommunications department.

If your telephone does not have the correct features for your calling needs, please consult with the telecommunications department.

Telephone Tones

Call Waiting Tone

A single short burst of tone heard through the loudspeaker during conversation indicates you have a call waiting. This tone is repeated once after ten seconds.

Ring Again Tone
A short burst of tone heard through the loudspeaker telling you the called station is now free.

Error Tone
Fast, busy tone.

Volume Control

The loudness of any sound that comes through the loudspeaker may be increased or decreased. There are approximately eight different volume settings.

While the set is ringing:

- press either VOL UP or VOL DOWN and when the desired volume is reached
- press VOL UP and VOL DOWN keys simultaneously to lock the volume level.

Note: Volume control does not control loudness of sound coming through the handset.

Hold

Allows you to place a call on hold and, if you wish, place or receive another call.

To activate:

- ask party to wait
- press HOLD key

To retrieve:

- press DIRECTORY NUMBER key next to the flashing diamond

Listen on Hold
When placed on hold by another party, this enables you to place your handset in the cradle and use the loudspeaker to listen for the party to return.

To activate:

- you have been placed on hold
- press HOLD key

- hang up
- press DIRECTORY NUMBER key next to the flashing diamond
- listen for the party to reestablish the call

    To retrieve:

- lift handset
- press DIRECTORY NUMBER key next to the flashing diamond
- continue your conversation

Last Number Redial

Allows you to redial the last called number by pressing the # key instead of dialing the full number.

    To activate:

- lift handset
- press ##
- number is automatically dialed

Automatic Dial

Allows you to program one frequently used number to be automatically dialed by pressing a single key.

    To program:

- without lifting the handset, press AUTO DIAL key
- dial the number to be stored
- press AUTO DIAL key again

    To activate:

- lift handset
- press AUTO DIAL key

Call Pickup

Allows you to answer any ringing phone in your call pickup area.

    To activate:

- lift handset
- press CALL PICKUP key

    You are automatically connected to the call.

Call Transfer

Allows you to transfer any call (internal or external) to any number within the system.

To activate:

- press CONF3 key
- hear special dial tone
- dial extension
- when third party answers, announce call
- press CONF3 key again
- hang up

Three-way Call

Allows you to establish a three-way call within or outside the system.

To activate:

- dial the first person's number
- press CONF3 key
- hear special dial tone
- dial second person's number
- announce conference
- press CONF3 key again

All parties are connected.

Consultation Hold

Allows you to consult privately with a second person while the initial call is on hold. You may flip-flop between the two calls as needed.

To activate:

- press CONF3 key
- hear special dial tone
- dial number of second person
- consult privately
- flip-flop between the two calls by alternately pressing DIRECTORY NUMBER key and CONF3 key

Group Intercom

Allows you to call another person within your intercom group by dialing a two-digit code.

To place call:

- lift handset
- press GROUP INTERCOM key
- dial code of the person you wish to speak to

To receive call:

- hear ringing
- lift handset
- press GROUP INTERCOM key

Call Forward

Allows you to forward your calls to another station within the system.

To activate:

- press CALL FORWARD key
- dial five-digit extension where you want calls forwarded
- press CALL FORWARD key

To cancel:

- press CALL FORWARD Key

Intercom

Allows you to have a dedicated connection between yourself and one other person.

To activate:

- lift handset
- press INTERCOM key
- hear ringing, then silence
- deliver message

Note: A two-way conversation is possible if the called party lifts their handset.

If you are on a call:

- hear buzz through loudspeaker
- press INTERCOM key (first call is placed on hold automatically)
- respond to intercom call
- to return to first call, press DIRECTORY NUMBER key

Speed Call Long or Short

Allows a group of individuals to place a call by dialing a one- or two-digit code.

To program from the designated controller's telephone:

- without lifting the handset, press SPEED CALL key
- dial one- or two-digit code
- dial number to be assigned to that code
- press SPEED CALL key again

To place a call:

- lift handset
- press SPEED CALL key
- dial one- or two-digit code

Number is automatically dialed.

Call Waiting

Allows you to be notified and to answer a second call while on an established call.

To activate:

- hear CALL WAITING tone
- press CALL WAITING key (first call automatically placed on hold)
- you are connected to the second call
- to return to first call press DIRECTORY NUMBER key

Note:

- you may flip-flop between calls as desired

- to terminate either call, press the release key while connected to that call

Call Park

Allows you to park an existing call for retrieval at your set or any other telephone within the system.

To park:

- press CALL PARK key
- hear confirmation tone
- hang up

To retrieve:

- lift handset
- press CALL PARK key
- hear special dial tone
- dial five-digit extension where call was parked

You are connected with party.

To cancel:

- press DIRECTORY NUMBER key and CALL PARK is cancelled

Ring Again

Notifies you when a busy extension that you have called becomes free.

To activate:

- hear busy signal
- press RING AGAIN key
- hang up

To respond:

- hear distinctive ring
- lift handset
- press RING AGAIN key

Extension is automatically dialed.

To cancel:

- press RING AGAIN key

INTERNATIONAL CALLING

Making International Calls

If your company uses AT&T for their international long distance calls here is how you dial an international call:

011 + [country code] + [city code] + [telephone number]

Country and city codes for some commonly called locations are listed on the following pages. These codes are similar to area codes. They remain the same no matter what long distance company you use. If you are having trouble reaching an international telephone number, check the following:

- Does your company use AT&T for international long distance? Other long distance companies may require you to dial a different code to access their international long distance lines. Check with your telecommunications department, office manager, or long distance company representative.
- Your telephone may be restricted from making international long distance calls. Check with the person in your company responsible for phone system programming to find out if this is the problem.
- The city or country code may be incorrect. Some large cities have several codes—and codes sometimes change. Try to get the correct city code when you get the telephone number or check with your long distance operator.

International Country and City Codes

Argentina – 54
  Buenos Aires – 1
Australia – 61
  Melbourne – 3
  Sydney – 2
Austria – 43
  Innsbruck – 5222
  Vienna – 222

Belgium – 32
  Brussels – 2

Brazil – 55
  Brasilia – 61
  Rio de Janeiro – 21

Colombia – 57
  Bogota – 1

Denmark – 45
  Copenhagen – 1 or 2

Egypt – 20
  Cairo – 2
  Port Said – 66

France – 33
  Marseille – 91
  Nice – 93
  Paris – 13, 14 or 16

Germany, East – 37
  Berlin – 2

Germany, West – 49
  Bonn – 228
  Frankfurt – 69

Greece – 30
  Athens – 1

Ireland – 353
  Dublin – 1

Israel – 972
  Jerusalem – 2
  Tel Aviv – 3

Italy – 39
  Rome – 6

Japan – 81
  Osaka – 6
  Tokyo – 3
  Yokohama – 45

Kenya – 254
    Nairobi – 2

Korea – 82
    Seoul – 2

Mexico – 52
    Mexico City – 5

Netherlands – 31
    Amsterdam – 20

Philippines – 63
    Manila – 2

Poland – 48

Spain – 34
    Madrid – 1

Sweden – 46
    Stockholm – 8

Switzerland – 41
    Geneva – 22

United Kingdom – 44
    Edinburgh (Scotland) – 31
    Liverpool (England) – 51
    London – 1

INTERNATIONAL TIME ZONES

When making international calls it is important to be aware of daylight savings time, which will skew the following numbers on the chart by one hour unless the foreign country you are calling also has daylight savings.

When calling Japan and Australia, it may be easier to find the time by subtracting a number from U.S. time—but you must remember the time you get will be the next day in the country you are calling. To avoid this confusion, the times on this chart are positive numbers if the country is across the international dateline from the United States and negative only if the country is on the U.S. side of the dateline.

Find your time zone in the top row. Follow the column for that time zone down to the city you wish to call. Add or subtract the number listed from your current time to get the time in the distant city.

	Eastern (New York, Miami)	Central (Chicago, Dallas)	Mountain (Denver)	Western (Seattle, LA)
Amsterdam	+6	+7	+8	+9
Athens	+7	+8	+9	+10
Beijing	+13	+14	+15	+16
Beirut	+7	+8	+9	+10
Berlin	+6	+7	+8	+9
Bogota	0	+1	+2	+3
Buenos Aires	+2	+3	+4	+5
Cairo	+7	+8	+9	+10
Dublin	+5	+6	+7	+8
Frankfurt	+6	+7	+8	+9
Geneva	+6	+7	+8	+9
Havana	0	+1	+2	+3
Hong Kong	+13	+14	+15	+16
Istanbul	+7	+8	+9	+10
Jerusalem	+7	+8	+9	+10
London	+5	+6	+7	+8
Madrid	+6	+7	+8	+9
Manila	+13	+14	+15	+16
Mexico City	-1	0	+1	+2
Montreal	0	+1	+2	+3
Moscow	+8	+9	+10	+11
Nairobi	+8	+9	+10	+11
New Delhi	+10½	+11½	+12½	+13½
Paris	+6	+7	+8	+9
Rio de Janeiro	+2	+3	+4	+5
Rome	+6	+7	+8	+9
Stockholm	+6	+7	+8	+9
Sydney	+15	+16	+17	+18
Tel Aviv	+7	+8	+9	+10
Tokyo	+14	+15	+16	+17
Toronto	0	+1	+2	+3
Vancouver	-3	-2	-1	0
Vienna	+6	+7	+8	+9
Warsaw	+6	+7	+8	+9

Time Zones for Frequently Called United States Cities

Find your time zone in the top row. Follow the column for that time zone down to the city you wish to call. Add or subtract the number listed from your current time to get the time in the distant city.

	Eastern (New York, Miami)	Central (Chicago, Dallas)	Mountain (Denver)	Western (Seattle, LA)
Albany	0	+1	+2	+3
Albuquerque	-2	-1	0	+1
Anchorage	-5	-4	-3	-2
Atlanta	0	+1	+2	+3
Atlantic City	0	+1	+2	+3
Billings	-2	-1	0	+1
Birmingham	-1	0	+1	+2
Bismark	-1	0	+1	+2
Boise	-2	-1	0	+1
Boston	0	+1	+2	+3
Buffalo	0	+1	+2	+3
Burlington	0	+1	+2	+3
Charleston, SC	0	+1	+2	+3
Charleston, WV	0	+1	+2	+3
Charlotte	0	+1	+2	+3
Chicago	-1	0	+1	+2
Cincinnati	0	+1	+2	+3
Cleveland	0	+1	+2	+3
Columbus	0	+1	+2	+3
Concord	0	+1	+2	+3
Dallas/Fort Worth	-1	0	+1	+2
Denver	-2	-1	0	+1
Des Moines	-1	0	+1	+2
Detroit	0	+1	+2	+3
Duluth	-1	0	+1	+2
El Paso	-2	-1	0	+1
Fargo	-1	0	+1	+2
Flagstaff	-2	-1	0	+1
Hartford	0	+1	+2	+3
Honolulu	-5	-4	-3	-2
Houston	-1	0	+1	+2

	Eastern (New York, Miami)	Central (Chicago, Dallas)	Mountain (Denver)	Western (Seattle, LA)
Indianapolis	0	+1	+2	+3
Jacksonville	0	+1	+2	+3
Juneau	-5	-4	-3	-2
Kansas City	-1	0	+1	+2
Las Vegas	-3	-2	-1	0
Los Angeles	-3	-2	-1	0
Louisville	0	+1	+2	+3
Memphis	-1	0	+1	+2
Miami	0	+1	+2	+3
Minneapolis	-1	0	+1	+2
Nashville	-1	0	+1	+2
New Orleans	-1	0	+1	+2
Oklahoma City	-1	0	+1	+2
Omaha	-1	0	+1	+2
Orlando	0	+1	+2	+3
Philadelphia	0	+1	+2	+3
Phoenix	-2	-1	0	+1
Pittsburgh	0	+1	+2	+3
Portland, ME	0	+1	+2	+3
Portland, OR	-3	-2	-1	0
Providence	0	+1	+2	+3
Reno	-3	-2	-1	0
Richmond	0	+1	+2	+3
Sacramento	-3	-2	-1	0
Saint Louis	-1	0	+1	+2
Salt Lake City	-2	-1	0	+1
San Antonio	-1	0	+1	+2
San Diego	-3	-2	-1	0
San Francisco	-3	-2	-1	0
Santa Fe	-2	-1	0	+1
Seattle	-3	-2	-1	0
Spokane	-3	-2	-1	0
Tampa	0	+1	+2	+3
Topeka	-1	0	+1	+2
Tucson	-2	-1	0	+1
Tulsa	-1	0	+1	+2
Washington, DC	0	+1	+2	+3
Wilmington	0	+1	+2	+3

INDEX